NEW Challenges

Liz Kilbey
Lindsay White

Workbook 2

Contents

My Skills

Vocabulary: Verbs

1 **Write the verbs under the correct pictures.**

cook count draw kiss play run sing swim touch ~~write~~

1 *write*

2 ______

3 ______

4 ______

5 ______

6 ______

7 ______

8 ______

9 ______

10 ______

Grammar: *can*

➤ Grammar Reference, page 95

☆ **2** **Choose the correct form of *can*.**

1 One ... deux ... three ... quatro? I *can*/(*can't*) count in English!
2 F-R-I-D-A-Y. I *can/can't* spell the day after Thursday.
3 Look! Spaghetti! I *can/can't* cook an Italian meal.
4 Can you say the alphabet backwards in English? Y ... Z ... X ... W ... No, I *can/can't!*
5 Can you sing in French? Yes, I *can/can't*.
6 What can your dog do? She *can/can't* run, swim and jump.

☆☆ **3** **Put the words in order.**

1 can / 100 / swim / metres / they
They can swim 100 metres.
2 can / my / English / I / talk / in / family / about
______
3 touch / your / tongue / elbow / your / can / with / you / ?
______
4 it / metres / four / jump / can't
______
5 her / her / elbow / can't / nose / with / touch / she
______
6 say / can / French / what / you / in / ?
______

☆☆☆ **4** **Write the questions and short answers.**

1 Anna / draw / a horse? ✓
Can Anna draw a horse? Yes, she can.
2 Greg / write / in French? ✗
______
3 Dan / sing / well? ✓
______
4 Jan and Eric / play the piano? ✓
______
5 you and your sister / say 'hello' in Spanish? ✗
______
6 your cat / swim? ✗
______

5 Look at the pictures. Write sentences with *can* or *can't*.

1 *She can't cook.*

2 ______

3 ______

4 ______

Listening

02 6 Listen and write the numbers under the pictures.

a

☐

b

☐

c

☐

d

☐

e

☐

f

1

Your Turn

7 What can you do? Write three sentences.

1 ______
2 ______
3 ______

8 What can't you do? Write three sentences.

1 ______
2 ______
3 ______

Writing: Capital letters

9 Circle and correct the words which have a capital letter.

America
omelette(america)aeroplanemondaychesspablodogjanuaryenglishk

10 Write the dialogues with capital letters where necessary.

1 **A** what can i see in madrid?
B the prado museum
A What can I see in Madrid?
B The Prado Museum

2 **A** can you read this email from turkey?
B no, i can't. ask mr harris – he can speak Turkish
______
______

3 **A** today, wednesday 22nd june, is my birthday.
B happy birthday, clare!
______
______

4 **A** can we see the eiffel tower in paris?
B yes, you can, and you can climb it. you can see all the city.
______
______

B Street Survey

Vocabulary: Objects

1 **Complete the words under the pictures.**

1 *skateboard*   2 l _ _ t _ p

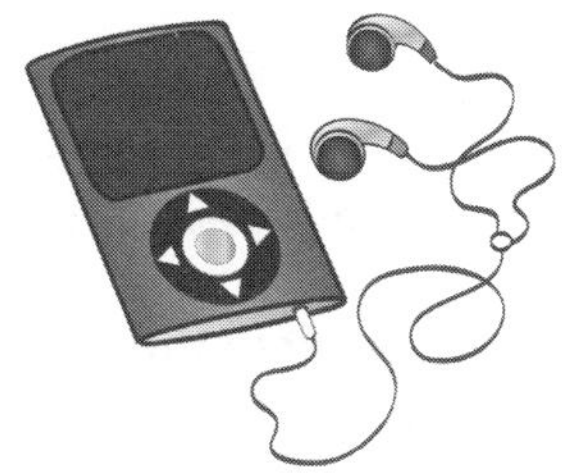

3 g _ _ t a _   4 _ _ g _ _ _ l c _ _ _ _ a   5 d _ _ _ s   6 _ o b _ _ e _ _ o n e   7 M _ 3 p _ _ _ e r

Reading

2 **Read and match.**

(a)

3

(b)

☐

(c)

☐

What have you got in your bag?

1 I've got four things in my bag. I've got my mobile phone. It hasn't got a camera. I've got a digital camera but I haven't got it in my bag. I've got my laptop and an English book. I can read it with a dictionary! I've got my electric guitar.

2 I can't count the things in my bag! I've got my acoustic guitar. I haven't got my laptop – it's at home. I've got my mobile phone, an MP3 player and a digital camera. I've got a photo of my boyfriend.

3 In my bag I've got an aeroplane and a musical instrument. I haven't got a phone but I've got a digital camera and a photo of my dog. My brother's got a skateboard in his bag.

Grammar: *have got/has got*

➤ Grammar Reference, page 95

☆ **3 Find and correct the mistakes. One sentence is correct.**

1 She ~~have~~ *has* got a new mobile.
2 My dad haven't got an MP3 player.
3 You hasn't got a skateboard.
4 What can you got in your bag?
5 She hasn't got a pet.
6 We hasn't got a garden.
7 Have he got a guitar?

☆☆ **4 Complete the sentences with the correct form of *have got*.**

1 We can't play the song. We *haven't got* our guitars here.
2 Listen! I ________ ________ an English song on my MP3 player.
3 What ________ the cat ________ ?
4 ________ Ben and Lulu ________ skateboards? ________ , they have.
5 ________ Bella ________ a boyfriend? No, she ________ .
6 I can't ring you. I ________ ________ a mobile.
7 Look! We ________ ________ pictures of the group.

☆☆☆ **5 Write sentences with the correct form of *have got*.**

1 Kathy / pet?
Has Kathy got a pet?
2 my sister and I / no digital cameras
My sister and I haven't got digital cameras.
3 I / piano
____
4 Zara and Lily / guitars
____
5 Miss Offord / car
____
6 you / a mobile phone?
____
7 Rose / a laptop?
____
8 my dad / no skateboard
____

Your Turn

6 Write six sentences with the correct form of *have/has got*. Use the people in Box A and the things in Box B or your own ideas.

A	B
my mum/dad	car
my teacher	mobile
my pet	guitar
my friend	pet
me	brown eyes

1 *My mum hasn't got brown eyes.*
2 ________
3 ________
4 ________
5 ________
6 ________
7 ________

Writing: Apostrophes

7 Write the full form of the underlined contractions.

1 They've got green eyes. *They have*
2 She's ten years old. ________
3 He can't make a pizza. ________
4 Mr and Mrs Dawson haven't got a son. ________
5 We're in Class 3B. ________
6 Ivan's got a photo of Cristiano Ronaldo on his phone. ________

8 Put the apostrophes in the paragraph where necessary.

I'm good at music. Ive got a guitar and I can sing well. My friends good at music but she cant sing. She can play the piano and shes got drums. The drums arent acoustic, theyre electric.

C Quiz Time

Listening

03 **1 Listen and match the questions (1–6) with the answers (a–f).**

1	*b*	a)	2016
2		b)	~~96 metres~~
3		c)	Bart Simpson's mum
4		d)	Poland and Slovakia
5		e)	three
6		f)	water

Grammar: Question Words

➤ Grammar Reference, page 95

☆ **2 Complete the question words.**

1 H *o* *w* tall is the Eiffel Tower in Paris?
2 W _ _ _ is New Year's Eve?
3 W _ _ lives in Buckingham Palace?
4 W _ _ _ _ are the Rocky Mountains?
5 W _ _ _ is an omelette?

☆ **3 Match the questions (1–5) in Exercise 2 with the answers a–e).**

a North America
b Queen Elizabeth II
c 31st December
d eggs
e ~~324 metres~~ *1*

☆ **4 Put the words in order to make questions. Guess the answers then check at the bottom of the page.**

1 is / Day / May / when / ?
When is May Day?
2 many / are / how / in / February / days / ?
____
3 the / is / equator / where / ?
____
4 the / main / what / are / of / water / ingredients / ?
____
5 is / Lisa / who / Simpson / ?
____

☆☆☆ **5 Write the questions.**

1 **A** be / Statue of Liberty?
Where is the Statue of Liberty?
B New York.
2 **A** be / Moriarty?
____
B Sherlock Holmes' enemy
3 **A** be / Guy Fawkes Night?
____
B 5th November
4 **A** be / the Mona Lisa?
____
B a famous picture
5 **A** legs / insects / have got?
____

Your Turn

6 Use the words in the box and the prompts to write questions. Then answer them.

how long	what	when	where	~~who~~

1 your favourite singer?
Who is your favourite singer? Leona Lewis.
2 your journey to school?
____
3 your favourite meals?
____
4 your birthday?
____
5 your favourite place?
____

Writing: Question marks

7 Put a question mark at the end of the questions and a full stop at the end of the sentences.

1 What is your name*?*
2 When the sun shines, I'm happy
3 Who can kiss their elbow
4 What a nice boy
5 How many students are in your class

Exercise 4 answers

1 1st May
2 28 or 29
3 0° latitude
4 hydrogen and oxygen
5 Bart Simpson's sister

D My Area

Vocabulary: Places

1 Where do you go? Complete the place names.

1 I want to buy a magazine.
n *e w s a g e n t*'s
2 I need to get some money.
b _ _ _
3 I want to buy some food for dinner.
s _ _ _ _ _ _ _ _ _ _
4 I want to do some aerobics.
g _ _

2 Match the words (1–8) and (a–h).

1 bowling — e) alley
2 clothes
3 ice
4 post
5 shopping
6 snack
7 sports
8 swimming

a) shop
b) centre
c) office
d) centre
e) alley
f) rink
g) pool
h) bar

Grammar: *there is/are* with *some* and *any*

▶ Grammar Reference, page 96

☆ **3 Match the questions (1–6) with the answers (a–f).**

1 Is there a supermarket in your street? *c*
2 Are there any cinemas in town? ___
3 Is there a park near here? ___
4 What shops are there? ___
5 Are there any shops in Wallace Road? ___

a) No, there aren't. And there aren't any sports centres.
b) Yes, there are. There's a newsagent's and a supermarket.
c) ~~Yes, there is.~~
d) There are some clothes shops and there's a computer games shop.
e) Yes, there is. You can play football there.

☆☆ **4 Complete the questions and answers. Use *is/isn't, are/aren't, there, any, some, yes* and *no*.**

1 A *Is* there an ice rink in town?
B Yes, there *is* .
2 A ________ there ________ parks near your house?
B No, ________ aren't.
3 A Is ________ a good place to eat?
B Yes, there ________ ________ nice snack bars in the shopping centre.
4 A ________ there a newsagent's near you?
B No, ________ ________ .

☆☆☆ **5 Write sentences with the opposite meaning.**

1 There's a gym.
There isn't a gym.
2 There aren't any clothes shops.
____
3 There isn't a snack bar.
____
4 We can't go swimming. There isn't a swimming pool.
____
5 There are some dogs in the park.
____
6 We can go to town. There's a bus.
____

Your Turn

6 Complete the paragraph. Make it true for your area.

I live in ________________ . Near my home, there's a ________________ but there isn't a ________________ . There are some ________________ but there aren't any ________________ . I can ________________ in the ________________ .

Writing: Commas

7 Put commas in the correct places in the paragraph.

I'm Ellen Mary Ellis. I live in a small town near Cambridge. In my town, there isn't a gym a swimming pool or a bowling alley. There is a park. We can play football basketball and ride our bikes there. In Cambridge, there are cinemas big shopping centres and sports centres. On Friday Saturday and Sunday we can cycle to Cambridge and swim.

E My House

Vocabulary

1 Complete the words (1–8) and match them with the pictures (a–h).

1 *b o o k c a s e* [*c*]
2 c _ a _ r [ ]
3 c _ _ p _ _ _ r [ ]
4 c _ p _ _ _ r d [ ]
5 _ e _ k [ ]
6 l _ _ _ [ ]
7 _ a _ l _ [ ]
8 t _ l _ _ _ _ _ _ n [ ]

a
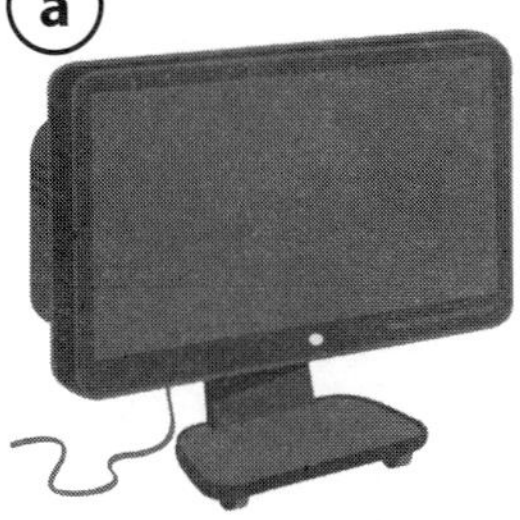

b

c

d

e

f
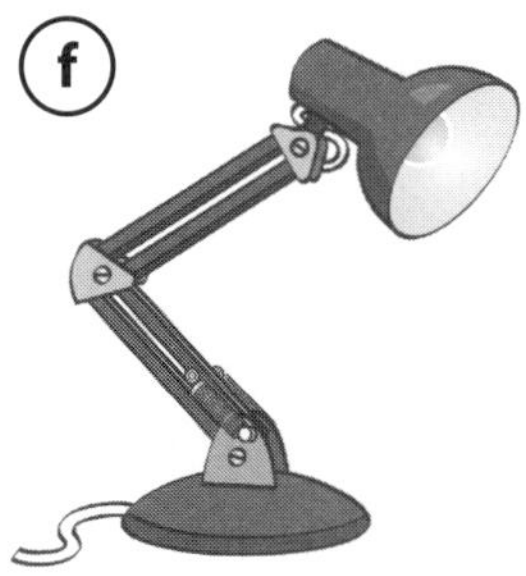

g

h
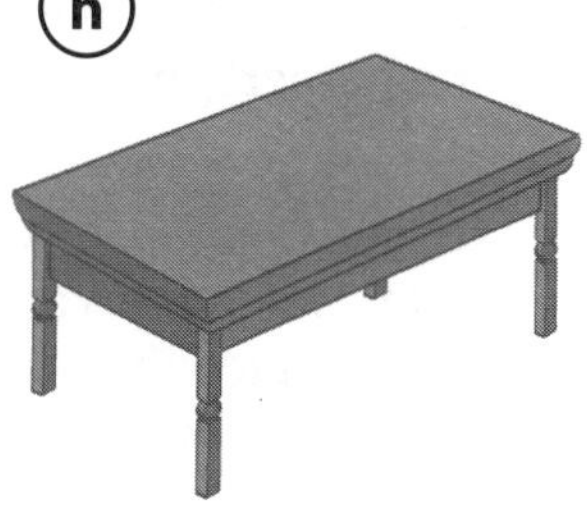

2 Put the furniture and things in the rooms.

armchair bath bed bookcase
chair cooker cupboard desk
fridge shower sink sofa table
toilet wardrobe washing machine

bathroom	bedroom
kitchen	**living room**

Listening

04 **3** Three people are talking about their living rooms. Listen and match.

a

2

b

[ ]

c

[ ]

Grammar: Comparatives and Superlatives

➤ Grammar Reference, page 96

☆ **4 Choose the correct answers.**

1 The laptop is (*smaller than*) /*the smallest* the other computer.
2 This is *the more expensive/the most expensive* television in the shop.
3 Stella's room is *more nice/nicer* than her sister's.
4 I've got my *best/better* pictures on my phone.
5 My phone is *the cheapest/most cheap* you can buy.
6 My bedroom is small, dark and cold. It's *the worst/bad* room in our house!
7 I hate this music! This is the *more boring/most boring* band I've ever heard.
8 This is the *less exciting/least exciting* computer game in the world.

☆☆ **5 Write sentences with comparative and superlative adjectives.**

1 our house / old / your house
Our house is older than your house.
2 our parents' bedroom / small / in the flat
Our parents' bedroom is the smallest in the flat.
3 my brother's laptop / good / my laptop
____
4 the black armchair / less comfortable / in the living room
____
5 the kitchen / busy / room in our house
____
6 Evan's hobby / interesting / Pete's
____
7 the lamp / not more expensive / thing in my bedroom
____
8 Sally / nice / girl I know
____
9 My top score in this game / good / yours
____

☆☆☆ **6 Look at the information about laptops and write sentences.**

	Alpha 	**Beta** 	**Gamma** 
price	300	500	600
fast	*	**	***
kilogrammes	3.00 kg	2.5 kg	2.00 kg

1 Alpha cheap
The Alpha is the cheapest.
2 Beta/Gamma expensive
The Gamma is more expensive than the Beta.
3 Gamma fast
____
4 Beta / Gamma / slow
____
5 Alpha / not expensive
____
6 Alpha / heavy
____
7 Gamma / not heavy
____

Your Turn

7 Write about your room. Use the questions to help you and your own ideas.

- What furniture have you got?
- What things have you got?
- What can you do there?

____
____
____
____

Writing: Punctuation

8 Put capital letters, apostrophes, question marks and commas in the correct places in the paragraph.

I'
~~i~~ve got a laptop. its very old slow and heavy. i cant watch films on it. my brother jacks got a new laptop. his is fast and it isnt heavy. have you got a computer whats it like

Module 1 Our World

Get Ready

Vocabulary: Hobbies and interests

1 Look at the information about a Youth Club. Write the words for activities.

•BRIXHAM • YOUTH • CLUB•

1 c *h e s s*

2 r _ _ _ _ vg

3 p _ _ _ _ _ _ _ _ _ y

4 s _ _ _ _ _ e

5 s _ _ _ t

6 m _ _ _ c

7 a _ _

8 s _ _ _ _ _ _ _ _ _ _ _ g

9 f _ _ _ _ _ n

10 d _ _ _ _ _ g

Listening

05 **2** Listen and complete the notes.

	 Andy	 Kelly	 Jack
age:	1 *14*	4 ______	9 ______
from:	*Manchester*	5 ______	*Ireland*
likes:	*music and*	6 ______ and	10 ______ and
	2 ______	7 ______	11 ______
isn't into:	3 ______	8 ______	12 ______

3 Complete the names of places in London. Use the words in the box.

PLACES IN LONDON
Bridge Circus Garden
Palace ~~Parliament~~ Royal

1 The Houses of *Parliament*
2 Covent ______
3 Tower ______
4 Buckingham ______
5 The ______ Observatory
6 Piccadilly ______

1 Vocabulary and Grammar

Vocabulary: Communication

1 **Write the words for kinds of communication.**

card	chatroom	~~email~~	mobile	landline	text

1 *email*

2 ________

3 ________

4 ________

5 ________

6 ________

2 **What do you need? Write the words under the pictures, with *send* or *use*.**

~~cards~~	~~chatrooms~~	emails	instant messages	letters
texts	the Internet	mobile	social networking sites	

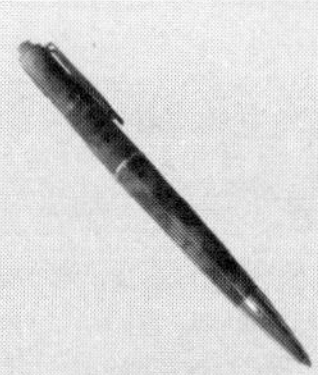

send cards
____

use chatrooms
____
____
____
____

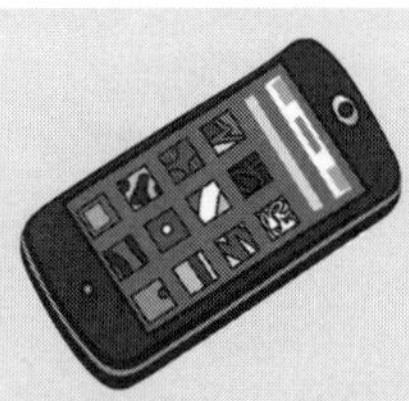

____
____

Grammar: Present Simple

➤ Grammar Reference, page 98

☆ **3** **Choose the correct words.**

1 I (*speak*)/*speaks* two languages.
2 We *have/has* five maths lessons every week.
3 I *don't/doesn't* like Monday mornings.
4 My brother *use/uses* our computer all the time.
5 My friends *don't/doesn't* use their home phones, but they *use/uses* their mobiles all the time.
6 My dad *don't/doesn't* use computers because he *hate/hates* them!

☆☆ **4** **Put the verbs in the correct form of the Present Simple.**

1 I *use* (use) the Internet every day.
2 My mum ________ (not like) emails but she ________ (love) writing letters.
3 All my friends ________ (like) texting.
4 I ________ (not read) newspapers but I ________ (like) magazines.
5 We ________ (go) shopping every Saturday.

5 Change the sentences to mean the opposite.

1 We *don't* like getting lots of homework.
2 My cousin ~~doesn't~~ speaks English.
3 I tidy my room every day.
4 My friends don't want to play computer games.
5 My mum likes loud music.
6 You live near my house.
7 Jack phones his girlfriend every day.
8 Ellie doesn't do her homework on the computer.

6 Write the adverbs in the correct order.

sometimes ~~always~~ usually never hardly ever often

(100%) *always* → ______ → ______ → ______ → ______ → ______ (0%)

7 Choose the correct adverbs.

1 It (*never*)/*often* snows in Jamaica.
2 Winter *sometimes/always* comes after autumn.
3 We *hardly ever/usually* go to school on Mondays.
4 I *sometimes/usually* speak English at school.
5 I *usually/never* brush my teeth in the morning.
6 My friends *hardly ever/usually* write letters.
7 I *never/often* go out at weekends.

8 Write true sentences. Use the verbs in the box or your own ideas.

do eat go speak watch ~~wear~~

1 (usually) *I usually wear jeans at the weekends.*
2 (never) ______
3 (hardly ever) ______
4 (sometimes) ______
5 (always) ______
6 (often) ______

9 Match the questions (1–5) and the answers (a–e).

1 Do you often get emails? [*c*]
2 How often do you use a computer? [ ]
3 Do you always walk to school? [ ]
4 Where do you have lunch? [ ]
5 Who do you send instant messages to? [ ]

a) My friends from school, and sometimes my pen friend.
b) At school.
c) No, not often.
d) Every day.
e) No, I sometimes cycle.

10 Complete the questions. Use the words in brackets.

1 'When *do you usually do* (you / usually / do) your homework?' 'After dinner.'
2 'How often ______ (your mum / use) the Internet?' 'Hardly ever.'
3 '______ (you / often / buy) new clothes?' 'No, I don't.'
4 '______ (your friends / use) chatrooms?' 'No, they don't.'
5 'How often ______ (your teachers / give) you homework?' 'Every day!'

Your Turn

11 Write questions, then answer them. Write sentences or short answers.

1 you / usually / send birthday cards to your friends?
Do you usually send birthday cards to your friends?
No, I usually forget!
2 how often / you / use your home phone?
______
3 your best friend / often / text you?
______
4 you / often / use the Internet?
______

2 Skills

Vocabulary: Personality adjectives

1 **Complete the adjectives.**

1 f *u n n y*
2 h _ _ _ - w _ _ _ _ _ g
3 h _ _ p _ _ l
4 _ _ iend _ _
5 h o _ _ _ t
6 l _ _ y
7 k _ _ d
8 m _ _ d y
9 o u t _ _ _ _ g
10 p _ t i _ _ t
11 s _ y
12 u n _ _ _ y
13 o _ g _ n _ s _ d

2 **Match the pictures with the correct adjectives from Exercise 1.**

1 *funny*

2 ______

3 ______

4 ______

5 ______

6 ______

Reading

3 **Read about Luke and Hannah and complete the text. Choose a), b) or c).**

Luke and Hannah are brother and sister. They get [1] *c* really well – in fact, they are [2] ______ friends! They go to the same school, and they have the same [3] ______ – music. Luke plays [4] ______ piano and Hannah plays the guitar.

Luke is very good [5] ______ science, but his favourite subject is maths. He's quiet [6] ______ he isn't shy. He [7] ______ be very funny. He's hard-working [8] ______ he's at school, but he is sometimes lazy [9] ______ home.

Hannah loves languages and she's interested [10] ______ geography, too. She's friendly and outgoing, and she's [11] ______ lots of friends. She is a good [12] ______ and she always helps her friends.

	a)	b)	c)
1	a) up	b) in	c) on
2	a) the best	b) best	c) better
3	a) interested	b) interest	c) interesting
4	a) –	b) the	c) a
5	a) at	b) on	c) in
6	a) because	b) and	c) but
7	a) can	b) does	c) is
8	a) and	b) then	c) when
9	a) –	b) at	c) in
10	a) in	b) of	c) at
11	a) has	b) is	c) got
12	a) listening	b) listener	c) listen

4 **Read the text in Exercise 3 again. Choose *Right* (a), *Wrong* (b) or *Doesn't Say* (c).**

1 Luke gets on well with Hannah.
(a) Right **b)** Wrong **c)** Doesn't Say
2 They go to different schools.
a) Right **b)** Wrong **c)** Doesn't Say
3 They play music together.
a) Right **b)** Wrong **c)** Doesn't Say
4 Luke always works hard.
a) Right **b)** Wrong **c)** Doesn't Say
5 Hannah likes going to different countries.
a) Right **b)** Wrong **c)** Doesn't Say
6 She is popular.
a) Right **b)** Wrong **c)** Doesn't Say

5 **Complete the dialogue. Choose correct replies for Cath. There are two extra replies.**

Sean What are you into, Cath?
Cath 1 *e*
Sean That's cool. Can you play an instrument?
Cath 2 __
Sean Me too, but I'm not very good. Is music your favourite subject at school?
Cath 3 __
Sean Do you want to be a musician?
Cath 4 __
Sean I want to be a teacher. But I'm not very patient!
Cath 5 __
Sean Well, thanks!

a) Yes, it is – but I like science too.
b) Maybe, but you're hard-working – that's a good start! And you get on with kids.
c) I can't play the guitar. Can you?
d) No, I don't. I want to be a doctor, I think. What about you?
e) I like fashion … and music.
f) Yes, school's okay.
g) Yes, I can. I play the guitar.

6 **Match the words from A and B and complete the sentences.**

Word Builder

A get x 3 go ~~look~~ wait

B ~~after~~ for on out to up

1 We're going on holiday. Can you *look after* my pets, please?
2 I like John. I ________ with him well.
3 I'm almost ready – please ________ me!
4 I ________ at 7 in the week, and at 9 at weekends.
5 I don't ________ out with my friends on school nights.
6 When you ________ know Laura she's really friendly and funny.

7 **Look at Sam's marks. Complete the description with *good*, *bad*, *at* or *in*.**

Sentence Builder

Sam Wallis	
Maths	100%
Geography	90%
Science	87%
English	40%
French	10%

Sam is very [1] *good* [2] ________ maths. He's really interested [3] ________ it. He's [4] ________ [5] ________ geography and science, too, but he's [6] ________ [7] ________ English – and he's very, very [8] ________ [9] ________ French!

Your Turn

8 **Complete the sentences. Use the words in the box or your own ideas.**

chess dancing fashion housework maths music remembering birthdays science singing ~~sleeping~~ spelling sport

1 I'm really good *at sleeping.*
2 I'm interested ________
3 I'm not very interested ________
4 I'm not very good ________
5 I'm bad ________
6 I'm very bad ________

3 Communication

Key Expressions: Preferences

1 Write the expressions under the correct pictures.

can't stand   don't like   don't mind   hate   like   ~~love~~

☺☺	☺	😐	☹	☹☹
love	______	______	______	______ ______

2 Read and listen to the conversation. Then complete the sentences with the correct form of the verbs in Exercise 1. Use each verb once.

06

Della Are you into sport, James?
James Yes, I am. I play football every week and I'm in the basketball team, too. What about you?
Della Well, I am not into football. But I play tennis sometimes. It's okay, I guess.
James So, what are you interested in?
Della Music. I play the piano.
James Wow! What kind of music do you usually play?
Della Classical and jazz – but jazz is my favourite. It's great. What kind of music do you like?
James Well not classical. Sorry, but I think it's horrible.
Della What about jazz? Do you like that?
James No, not really. I usually listen to rock or pop.

James [1] *loves* sport. Della [2] ______ ______ football but she [3] ______ ______ tennis.
Della [4] ______ classical music and she [5] ______ jazz. James [6] ______ classical music and he [7] ______ ______ jazz.

3 Read and listen to the conversation in Exercise 2 again. Write sentences with *a lot* and *very much*.

07

Sentence Builder

1 (James / sport) *James likes sport a lot.*
2 (Della / sport) ______
3 (Della / jazz) ______
4 (James / jazz) ______

Your Turn

4 Write true sentences.

1 I love ______
2 My friends and I don't mind ______
______
3 I like ______ a lot.
4 My friends can't stand ______
5 I don't like ______ very much.
6 My best friend hates ______

Vocabulary

5 Complete the dialogues with the expressions in the box.

anyway ~~Good idea~~ let's me too you sound like

A Let's get tickets for the rock concert. It's The Banjees.
B [1] *Good idea.* I'm really into their music.
A [2] ______ ! They're cool.

A Look! There's the new student. [3] ______ ask him to your party.
B You ask him. I'm shy.
A [4] ______ a ten-year-old!
B No, I don't! [5] ______ , I don't want to ask him.

Listening

08 **6 Listen to five dialogues and answer the questions. Choose a), b) or c).**

1 What's her mobile number?

a)	b)	c)
02871 634885	02871 634855	02871 638855
☐	☑	☐

2 What's his address?

a)	b)	c)
21 Cleys Road	21 Klees Road	21 Kleys Road
☐	☐	☐

3 What's her email address?

a)	b)	c)
sue@daz.com	sui@daz.com	sue@das.com
☐	☐	☐

4 When's her birthday?

a)	b)	c)
20th April 1996	12th April 1994	12th April 1996
☐	☐	☐

5 What's his name?

a)	b)	c)
Geoff Murphy	Jeff Murphy	Geff Murphy
☐	☐	☐

Reading Corner 1

1 Answer the questions.

1 What's your opinion of computers?

a) They're exciting.
b) I'm scared of them.
c) They're just a part of everyday life.

2 How often do you use the Internet?

a) hardly ever
b) sometimes
c) every day

3 Why do you use the Internet? (You can choose more than one answer.)

a) to find information
b) to talk to friends
c) to buy things
d) for fun (music, films, games, etc.)

4 Do you write a blog?

a) Yes, I do.
b) No, I don't.
c) No, but I like reading other people's blogs.

2 Answer the questions again – this time for your parents.

3 Choose the correct headings.

a) Goodbye, postcards!
b) Everyday equipment
c) How do they use it?
d) Teenagers and the Internet

1 ___d___

2 ______

Teenagers today are the first 'Internet children'. Computers are part of their lives, just like televisions, telephones and mobiles.

3 ______

A new survey shows that British teenagers use the Internet for about eight hours a week. Older people use the Internet to find information, to read the news or to shop online, but their children use the Internet to communicate with friends with email and instant messaging. More and more teenagers write their own blogs, too. Here's an amazing fact: someone starts a new blog every second!

4 ______

Bloggers usually write about their lives. They write about their interests and often list their favourite websites too. Some bloggers are away from home. Their friends and family can read their blogs and find out all their news. Blogs often have pictures on their pages. Sometimes the pictures are from mobile phones – then they are called moblogs! Of course, some blogs and moblogs are boring, but some can be great. ☺

4 Are these sentences about the text true (T) or false (F)?

The writer thinks …

1	computers aren't very exciting for teenagers.	T
2	older people don't use computers.	
3	teenagers mainly use the Internet to communicate.	
4	blogs aren't very popular with young people.	
5	blogs are usually boring.	

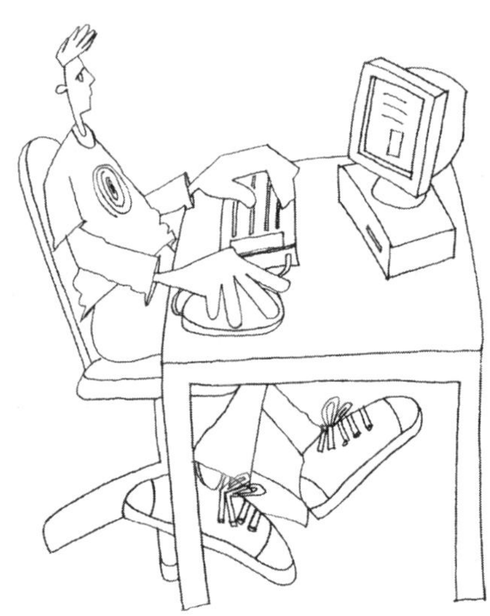

5 Read the blog and find the missing sentences.

a) There's only one problem ... shopping isn't part of the trip.
b) This is our second day here in Dublin.
c) It's a museum, but it is NOT boring.
d) We can try horse riding, climbing and cycling (on mountain bikes).
e) Then we watch TV or play games.
f) The weather isn't very good and we all feel sick.

Mayfield School Trip to Ireland

Kirstie Lamb's blog

Monday

Hi
1 __b__ . It's about a thousand years old and I love it! There are some beautiful old streets with interesting little shops, and the people are very friendly. My favourite place is 'Dublinia'. 2 _____ It's a really interesting place. You can walk through the streets of old Dublin, visit a house and even go round an old ship. Amazing! There are some great parks here too and I think the shopping centre is really good. 3 _____ :)
We're all fine.

Wednesday

We're at an activity centre now. 4 _____ It isn't a very big place, and it's in the middle of the countryside. We cook our own food and do the washing-up. :(In the evening we do our projects (I'm lucky because my project is this blog!). 5 _____ :) We go to bed early because we get really tired!

Friday

Now we're on the ferry. 6 _____ . :(:(
Only another three hours!

Language Check 1

Vocabulary

1 Find the odd one out.

land line (*text messages*) *phone* *mobile*

1 art chess fashion social network site
2 the Internet cards letters postcards
3 science sport fashion hobby
4 email chatrooms instant messages texts
5 friendly moody helpful honest
6 music hard-working outgoing patient
7 get up look after interested in wait for
8 amazing skateboarding reading dancing
9 untidy lazy angry funny
10 photography shy fantastic great

☐ / 10

2 Choose the correct words.

I sometimes look (after)/with my little brother.

1 Don't wait *after/for* me, I'm not ready.
2 She's my friend. I get *on/up* with her really well.
3 John wants to go out *after/with* my sister!
4 I get *for/up* really late at weekends!
5 Please look *after/with* my dog for me.

☐ / 5

Grammar

3 Rearrange the words to make sentences.

do / often / you / go / shopping / How / ?
How often do you go shopping?

1 homework / you / get / usually / do / when / maths / ?
______
2 ever / newspapers / we / hardly / read
______
3 snow / in / your / does / it / country / often / ?
______
4 usually / I / don't / school / walk / to
______

☐ / 4

4 Complete the conversations with the correct form of the verbs in brackets, or short answers.

A Where *do* you *live* ? (live)
B I [1] ______ in Manchester, but my sister [2] ______ in London. (live)
A [3] ______ you and your friends often ______ letters? (write)
B No, we [4] ______ .
A Where [5] ______ your brother ______ to school? (go)
B He [6] ______ to school. (not go) He [7] ______ to university. (go)
A What kind of music [8] ______ you ______ ? (like)
B Rock. I [9] ______ pop. (not like)
A When [10] ______ your parents ______ home in the evening? (come)
B They [11] ______ home at about six. (come)

☐ / 11

Key Expressions

5 Write the underlined words by the correct picture.

Tania likes music. She doesn't mind dancing. She hates football. She loves chocolate. She can't stand coffee. She doesn't like dogs.

☺☺ *chocolate*
☺ 1 ______
😐 2 ______
☹ 3 ______
☹☹ 4 ______
☹☹ 5 ______

☐ / 5

What's your score?

Module 1

☐ Vocabulary
☐ Grammar
☐ Key Expressions
☐ / 35

This is easy.
I need more practice.
This is difficult.

Module 2 Neighbours

Get Ready

Vocabulary: Jobs

1 **Complete the words for jobs (1–11), then match them with the correct pictures (a–k).**

1	d *e n t i* s t	*e*
2	e l e c t _ _ _ _ _ n	
3	h a i r _ _ _ _ _ _ _ r	
4	l _ _ _ y d _ _ _ _ _ r	
5	m e c _ _ _ _ _ c	
6	p _ _ _ _ _ e o _ _ _ _ _ _ _ r	
7	p _ _ m b _ _	
8	s _ _ _ _ _ _ _ _ r y	
9	s h _ _ a _ _ _ _ _ _ _ _ n t	
10	_ _ x _ d _ _ _ _ _ r	
11	v _ _	

09 **2** **Listen to Mark and write true (T) or false (F).**

1	Mark and Jack live in London.	*T*
2	They don't like computers.	
3	They often play sport.	
4	They have an unfriendly neighbour.	
5	Mark is good at science.	
6	Emma is a helpful neighbour.	

Your Turn

3 **What are your neighbours like? Write six sentences.**

____

____

____

____

____

____

4 Vocabulary and Grammar

Vocabulary

1 Match the verbs (1–5) and the words (a–e).

1	do	**a)**	the cooking
2	speak	**b)**	a meal
3	make	**c)**	an exam
4	do	**d)**	a language
5	study for	**e)**	your homework

2 Complete the sentences. Use the words in the box.

accents	bilingual	~~grandparents~~	originally	typical

1 My *grandparents* are my parents' parents.
2 We all speak English but we have different ____________ .
3 Pasta is a ____________ Italian meal.
4 My dad can speak two languages. He's ____________ .
5 We're British but our family is ____________ from Poland.

3 Complete the text with words from Exercise 2.

A Summer Festival

Every summer there is a big festival in London. It's called the Notting Hill Festival.

[1] *Grandparents* , parents and children dance together in the street. About one million people from many different countries enjoy the festival every year – you can hear many different languages and [2] ____________ . Some of these people are visitors to Britain, but many are Londoners. Some of the children are [3] ____________ – they speak English at school and other languages at home.

The music and dances are [4] ____________ from the Caribbean. A lot of the food is [5] ____________ Caribbean food. There's only one problem: the weather is British!

Grammar: Present Continuous

➤ Grammar Reference, page 99

☆ **4 Look at the picture in Exercise 3. Complete the sentences in the Present Continuous.**

1 Look! The people *are dancing* (dance) in the street!
2 What ____________ (they / wear)?
3 Who ____________ (play) the music?
4 The little girl ____________ (enjoy) the Festival.
5 The dancers ____________ (not / wear) typical British clothes!

Grammar: Present Simple and Present Continuous

➤ Grammar Reference, page 100

☆ **5 Choose the correct form of the verbs.**

1 Every summer, people (*travel*) /*are travelling* to London for the festival.
2 *Do you usually go/Are you usually going* to the festival?
3 Listen! *They play/They're playing* the drums!
4 Can you see my sister? *She dances/She's dancing* in the street.
5 I *don't often dance/am not often dancing* – but this is fun!
6 They *always play/are always playing* very loud music.
7 Look at that woman! *She wears/She's wearing* amazing clothes!

☆☆ **6** **Complete the description with the verbs (a–h).**

a) are playing
b) walk
c) go
d) is playing
e) dance
f) loves
g) play
h) 's having

These men [1]___*c*___ to the festival every year. They [2]________ round the streets and [3]________ their music. They often [4]________ , too. Everybody [5]________ them. They [6]________ their instruments now. One man [7]________ a very big drum. He [8]________ a great time.

☆☆☆ **7** **Complete the text with the correct form of the verbs in brackets.**

Sarah [1]___*teaches*___ (teach) in a big London school. Many of her students [2]__________ (speak) English at school and a different language at home. She often [3]__________ (help) them with their English, but they also [4]__________ (learn) from their friends.
Today is Monday. It's 10 o'clock and Sarah [5]__________ (teach) science. Two of the students are from other countries and they [6]__________ (not speak) English very well. At the moment, a special teacher [7]__________ (help) them. She [8]__________ (explain) some new words to them.

☆ **8** **Complete the questions.**

1 Listen! What ___*are they singing*___ (they / sing)?
2 __________ (you / know) the answer?
3 What language __________ (they / usually / speak)?
4 What's funny? Why __________ (you / laugh)?
5 What __________ (you / look for)? Can I help?

☆☆ **9** **Make questions for the answers. Use the correct form of the verbs in the box.**

sit speak ~~go~~ watch do live

1 **Q** Why has your brother got his guitar? Where ___*is*___ he ___*going*___ ?
A Band practice.
2 **Q** ________ they ________ in Birmingham?
A No, they're Londoners.
3 **Q** Why ________ you ________ on the sofa?
A Because I'm tired.
4 **Q** What ________ you ________ ?
A *The Simpsons*. Come and watch it with me!
5 **Q** How many languages ________ he ________ ?
A Two. English and German.
6 **Q** What ________ she ________ ?
A Her homework, I think.

Reading

1 Complete the text. Choose a), b) or c).

Do you like travelling? Do you [1] ___c___ to visit different countries? Well, now you can see the world from your own home. You just need the Internet! Virtual travellers [2] ______ need tickets, so their journeys are free! They can go round the world in an afternoon or stay in their neighbourhood. They have fun and they [3] ______ never tired!

Would you like to see London? There are cameras in all the streets. What's [4] ______ in Trafalgar Square? Cars, taxis and buses are moving slowly round the square. People [5] ______ walking in and out of buildings, up and down steps, and round and round the statues. Just click on the screen and watch. Sometimes you can control the camera.

Would you like to go to the country, or a beach? Create your own virtual holiday – choose from a long list of exciting and wonderful places. Maybe you [6] ______ make a decision – don't worry, go to all of them!

And when you really go out, smile – because someone [7] ______ watching you!

Trafalga Square

	a)	b)	c)
1	a) wants	b) wanting	c) want
2	a) don't	b) aren't	c) haven't
3	a) is	b) are	c) be
4	a) happening	b) happens	c) happen
5	a) do	b) have	c) are
6	a) don't	b) can't	c) aren't
7	a) is	b) are	c) be

2 Choose a heading for the text.

a) Relax and Travel ☐
b) Plan Your Next Holiday ☐
c) The Computer Game for Travellers ☐

3 Match the definitions with words or phrases from the text.

1 not real – on a computer! (line 5) v i r t u a l
2 the area near my home. (line 9) _ _ _ _ _ _ _ _ _ _ _ _ _
3 a good time (line 9) _ _ _
4 direct (verb) (line 20) _ _ _ _ _ _ _
5 make (line 22) _ _ _ _ _ _
6 decide (line 25–6) _ _ _ _ _ _ _ _ _ _ _ _

Your Turn

4 Imagine there's a camera in the classroom. You and your partner are watching. What's happening?

____
____
____
____
____
____
____
____
____
____
____
____
____
____

Vocabulary

5 Complete the dialogues. Choose a), b) or c).

1 Would you like to see London?
- (a) That's a good idea!
- b) Yes, I do.
- c) Yes, I love it.

2 How often do you use the Internet?
- a) Yes, I'm using it now.
- b) Every day.
- c) Yes, I do.

3 What does he do?
- a) He works with computers.
- b) He's using a computer.
- c) Yes, he does.

4 Do you go to work?
- a) By bus.
- b) No, I'm a student.
- c) No, I'm going to town.

5 Are you playing a game?
- a) Yes, it's brilliant.
- b) Yes, sometimes.
- c) *The Sims.*

6 Do you like travelling?
- a) That's a good idea.
- b) By plane.
- c) Yes, it's great.

6 Complete the sentences. Choose a), b) or c).

1 My dog is __*b*__ old now.
a) being b) getting c) having

2 Children grow ________ – then they are adults.
a) up b) old c) tall

3 Does your brother go to ________ ?
a) job b) office c) work

4 I always ________ when I play chess!
a) fail b) lose c) fall

5 Wow! This picture is very ________ !
a) real b) really c) realistic

6 When you want to use the CD ROM, ________ on 'START'.
a) click b) touch c) press

7 Write the words.

1 We feel this when we are sad. u *n h a p p y*
2 This means 'not real'. i _ _ _ _ _ _ _ _ _
3 This is the opposite of 'unusual'. n _ _ _ _ _
4 This person lives near me. n _ _ _ _ _ _ _ _
5 When children grow up, they become these! a _ _ _ _ _
6 He or she is a person in a story. c _ _ _ _ _ _ _ _

8 Complete the sentences. Use expressions with *have*.

Word Builder

1 She's *having a party* .

2 It's ________________ .

3 They're ________________ .

4 He's ________________ .

9 Rewrite the sentences. Use the words in brackets.

Sentence Builder

1 Computers are useful because they can find information quickly. (so)
Computers can find information quickly, so they're useful.

2 I often play computer games, so I'm very good at them. (because)
____
____

3 I don't write many letters because I usually use the phone or email. (so)
____
____

4 Our computer's broken, so I can't do my homework. (because)
____
____

6 Communication

Vocabulary: Food and drink

1 **Write the words in the correct lists.**

burger ~~cola~~ hot dog kebab milk orange juice salmon tuna water

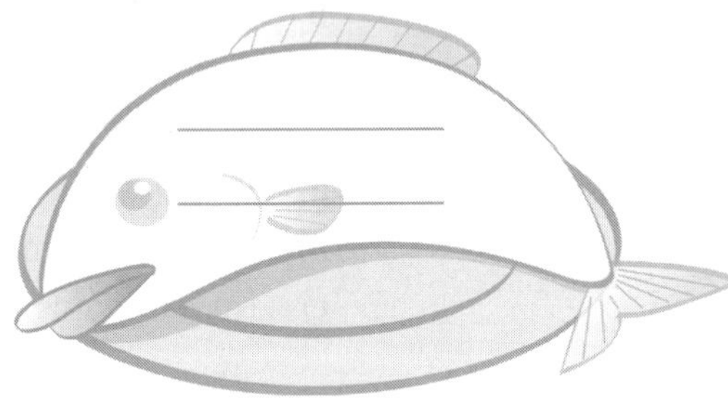

Key Expressions: At a café

2 **Complete the dialogue. Choose correct replies for the customer. There are two extra replies.**

Waiter Hello, welcome!
Customer 1 ___c___
Waiter Can I help you?
Customer 2 ________
Waiter Vegetable or meat?
Customer 3 ________
Waiter And what would you like to drink?
Customer 4 ________
Waiter Okay. Is that all?
Customer 5 ________
Waiter You're welcome.

a) An orange juice, I think. No, can I have a cola?
b) Yes, please.
c) Hi. Thanks.
d) Yes, I'd like a kebab, please.
e) Yes, you can.
f) Oh, meat, please.
g) Yes, thank you.

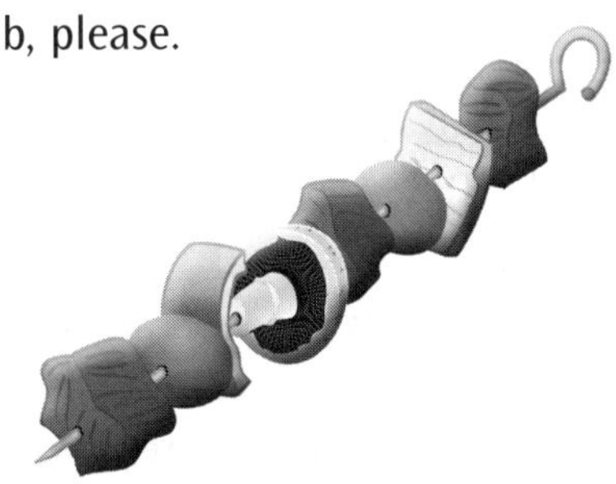

3 **Complete the dialogue. Write one word in each gap.**

Waiter Hello, ___can___ I ________ you?
Kate Yes, ________ . I ________ ________ a cheese salad, ________ .
Sam And ________ I ________ a hot dog, ________ ?
Waiter Okay. And what ________ you ________ ________ ________ ?
Sam I ________ ________ an orange juice, ________ .
Kate And a cola ________ me, ________ .

Listening

4 Listen and tick the correct orders.

1

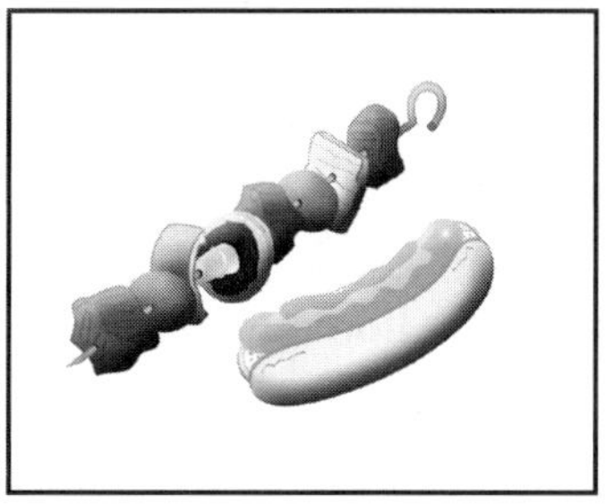

a) ☐

b) ☐

c) ☑

2

a) ☐

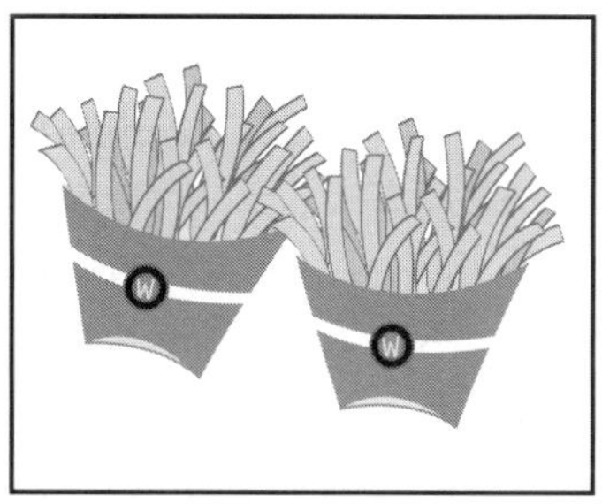

b) ☐

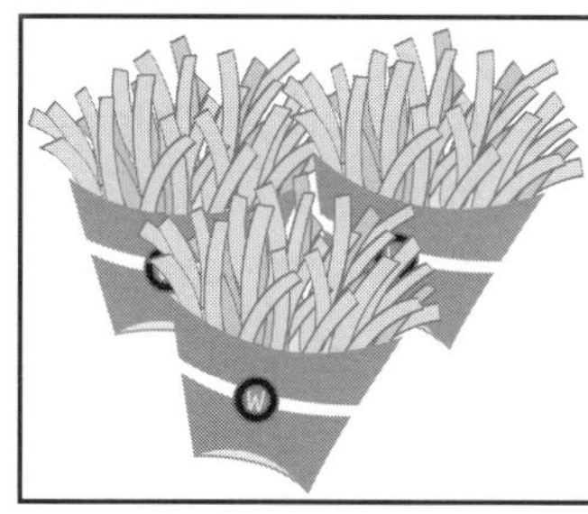

c) ☐

3

a) ☐

b) ☐

c) ☐

4

a) ☐

b) ☐

c) ☐

5 Listen and complete the information.

Customer's name:	*Jane*
Phone number:	
Address:	

Writing Challenge 1

1 **Read the email. Choose the correct answers.**

To: Class B

From: e-friends

Subject: Introduction to e-friends
Date: 3rd November

Hi!
Welcome to *e-friends*! Now you can make new friends around the world and learn more about their lives.

Your first e-friends are some students in Peru, South America! This is their address:

englishclass@ayacucho.com

They are waiting for your first email. Tell them about some or all of these things:

your class and your school
your interests
your town

Ask them some questions about their school and their lives.

This is a great chance for you – enjoy it!

Best wishes and good luck

Jenny and everyone at *e-friends*

1 Who is the message from?
   a) some students in Peru
   (b) an organisation called *e-friends*
   c) Class 6
2 What's it about?
   a) Peru
   b) travelling
   c) contacting new people
3 Who's going to write the next message?
   a) *e-friends*
   b) Class B
   c) some students in Peru
4 What are they going to write about?
   a) their lives
   b) Peru
   c) *e-friends*

2 **Choose the correct words.**

1 You can meet new people (*and*)/*but* learn about their lives.
2 This is a great way to learn about the world *so*/*because* you make friends at the same time.
3 I don't speak Spanish *and*/*but* my friends in Peru speak English.
4 We've got a computer at home *so*/*because* I can send emails easily.
5 I'd like to go to Peru one day. I'd like to go to Brazil, *so*/*too*.
6 I want to know about the country *and*/*too* the people.

3 **Complete the reply. Use *and* (x 2), *but* (x 3), *so*, *because* or *too*.**

Hi!

I'm one of your new e-friends!

I'm fourteen [1] *and* I live in a city called Hereford. It's in England, [2]_____ it's a great place. Maybe you can find it on a map.

I go to a big school. It has nearly 1,000 students [3]_____ the classes aren't very big. There are twenty people in mine. I study nine subjects. My favourite subject is geography, [4]_____ I want to hear all about Peru! I like languages, [5]_____ . I study French and German [6]_____ I don't study Spanish – sorry!

I'm into music, especially heavy metal and rock. I can't play a musical instrument [7]_____ I can sing. What about you?
I can't write any more now [8]_____ my mum's calling me. Please write back soon!

Your Turn

4 **Write your message to Peru!**

Understanding Grammar: *a, an* or *the*

➤ Grammar Reference, page 101

☆ **1 Choose the correct words.**

My friend Dave has got [1]*a/an/the* electric guitar. He plays in [2]*a/an/the* band. There's [3]*a/an/the* drummer and [4]*a/an/the* singer, too. [5]*A/An/The* band's name is Elephant. They practise every Saturday in [6]*a/an/the* old building in [7]*a/an/the* drummer's garden. [8]*A/An/The* drummer's name is Ben and he wants to be [9]*a/an/the* rock star.

☆☆ **2 Find and correct one mistake in each sentence.**

There's ~~the~~ *a* skateboarding park in our town, and there's a leisure centre too. I never go to a leisure centre because it's very expensive, but I often go to the skateboarding park. It's a amazing place and we always have a good time there. We've also got a really good cinema in town and my friend and I often go to see the film there. We'd like to go to concerts but we haven't got the concert hall in our town.

☆☆☆ **3 Complete the information about your house or flat.**

I live in a small house. It's got a kitchen, a sitting room, two bedrooms and a bathroom.

house or flat? *I live in* ______ *It's got* ______

______

what's it like? ______

______

______

______

favourite room? *My favourite room is* ______

what's in it? *There's* ______

______

______

4 Complete the sentences with *a*, *an*, *the* or nothing (–).

1 We usually go to ___*a*___ snack bar and have ______ lunch there.
2 There's ______ youth club in our town and I sometimes go there after ______ school.
3 My sister has ______ broken leg so she's in ______ hospital.
4 We've got two computers in our classroom. One of them is new, and it's great. ______ other one is old.
5 Do you ever have ______ breakfast in ______ bed?
6 I stay at ______ home on Saturday, but my friend Jo goes to ______ school.
7 I've got ______ old bike, but I usually travel by ______ car or ______ bus.
8 Look at those people. Is ______ man famous?

Language Check 2

Vocabulary

1 Who do they need? Complete the word for the job.

My cat's sick! vet

1 My hair is very untidy.
h _ _ _ _ _ _ _ _ _ _

2 I can't write letters and answer the phone at the same time! s _ _ _ _ _ _ _ _

3 The lights don't work!
e _ _ _ _ _ _ _ _ _ _

4 I've got a problem with my car.
m _ _ _ _ _ _ _

5 I don't feel very well.
d _ _ _ _ _

☐ / 5

2 Complete the sentences. Use expressions with *have*.

Every birthday I have a party and invite all my friends.

1 Tom's at the pool. He's having a ________ .
2 Everyone's laughing. They're having ________ .
3 I don't like baths, so I always have a ________ .
4 My mum usually does the cooking, and we have ________ at about 7 p.m.
5 It's one o'clock and I'm hungry. Let's have ________ .

☐ / 5

3 Write the word for the food or drink.

This brown drink is very popular. cola

1 This white drink is good for you. _ _ _ _
2 This round meal is from Italy! _ _ _ _ _
3 This is cold and delicious. _ _ _   _ _ _ _ _
4 Potatoes are _ _ _ _ _ _ _ _ _ s.
5 Apples and oranges are _ _ _ _ _ .
6 This food comes from the sea. _ _ _ _

☐ / 6

Grammar

4 Write the correct form of the verb in brackets. Use the Present Simple or Present Continuous.

Look, there's John! Where's he going (go)?

1 ________ you usually ________ (work) on Saturdays?
2 What's funny? Why ________ you ________ (laugh)?
3 I ________ ________ (wear) my new shoes today, but they aren't very comfortable.
4 Maisie always ________ (talk) in class. She's very noisy.
5 Look! Ben ________ ________ (not / study), he ________ (sleep)!

☐ / 5

5 Complete the sentences with *a, an, the* or nothing (–).

1 I've got ___*a*___ CD player and ________ MP3 player.
2 Do you usually go to ________ school by ________ bus?
3 I often buy ________ sandwich for ________ lunch.
4 There's ________ café and ________ restaurant near our school. ________ café is okay but I don't like ________ restaurant.

☐ / 9

Key Expressions

6 Complete the dialogue.

Waiter Can I ___*help*___ you?
Girl I'd [1]________ a pizza, [2]________ .
Waiter [3]________ would [4]________ like to drink?
Girl Can I [5]________ a bottle of water, please?

☐ / 5

What's your score?

Module 2

☐ Vocabulary
☐ Grammar
☐ Key Expressions
☐ / 35

This is easy.
I need more practice.
This is difficult.

Module 3 Life Stories

Get Ready

Vocabulary: Dates

1 **Match the dates in numbers (a–e) and in words (1–5).**

a) 14/8 b) 01/04 c) 30/03

d) 16/05 e) 09/09

1 The first of April *b*
2 The fourteenth of August
3 The ninth of September
4 The sixteenth of May
5 The thirtieth of March

2 **Write these dates in two ways.**

1 15/07/05 *15th July 2005*
the fifteenth of July two thousand and five
2 23/02/99 ______
3 02/06/76 ______
4 31/01/01 ______
5 12/04/52 ______

3 **Answer the questions.**

1 When does the year begin?
1st January
2 When does the year finish?
3 What's the date today?
4 When is your birthday?

Listening

12 **4** **May's grandmother is talking about her memories. Listen and choose the correct answers.**

1 When did Apollo 11 land on the Moon?
   (a) 20th July 1969 (circled)
   b) 20th June 1969
   c) 20th July 1960
2 May's grandmother remembers one special picture. Where was it?
   a) on TV
   b) in a magazine
   c) on a wall
3 What was in the picture?
   a) the astronauts
   b) the Earth
   c) the Moon
4 Who was the pilot?
   a) Neil Armstrong
   b) Buzz Aldrin
   c) Michael Collins
5 How many astronauts walked on the Moon?
   a) one
   b) two
   c) three

Your Turn

5 **Think of a special day from your past. Answer the questions. Write two or three sentences.**

What was the date? Where were you?
What happened?

7 Vocabulary and Grammar

Vocabulary

13 **1 Listen to six sentences. Write the verb in each sentence.**

1 s*aw* ______ 2 w______ 3 h______
4 m______ 5 t______ 6 w______

2 Write the infinitive form of the verbs in Exercise 1.

1 *see* 2 ______ 3 ______
4 ______ 5 ______ 6 ______

3 Match the two parts of these sentences.

1 Diego Maradona scored
2 John passed
3 My brother played
4 Kristen Stewart made
5 My dad started
6 We spent
7 John Lennon wrote
8 My sister married

a) his company in 2002.
b) the film *Eclipse* in 2010.
c) a lot of great songs.
d) her boyfriend last week.
e) our holidays next to the sea.
f) 33 goals for Argentina.
g) his music exam last week.
h) the guitar in the school concert.

4 Complete the sentences. Use the words in the box.

ago in last (x 2) when

1 My uncle went to Rome *last* year.
2 My grandmother wanted to be an astronaut ______ she was little.
3 Suzy finished her project a week ______ .
4 Tom went to Florida ______ 2005.
5 My brother started his first job ______ week.

Your Turn

5 Complete the sentences with true information.

1 I was born ______ years ago.
2 When I was little, I lived in ______ .
3 I was thirteen in ______ .
4 Last weekend, I ______ .
5 I started this exercise ______ ago.

Grammar: Past Simple

Grammar Reference, page 102

☆ **6 Complete the dialogues with the correct form of the verbs in brackets, or a short answer.**

1 A Where *were* (be) you yesterday?
B I ______ (be) at home.
I ______ (not / go) to school.
I ______ (go) to the dentist's.

2 A When ______ (you / move) to this town?
B We ______ (move) here in 2005.

3 A What time ______ (the film / finish) last night?
B It ______ (finish) at ten and we ______ (get) home at eleven.

4 A ______ (you and Joe / have) fun yesterday?
B Yes, we ______ .
We ______ (have) a great time!

7 Complete the dialogue. Write one word in each gap.

Adam Where [1] *were* you born, Rachel?
Rachel I [2] ______ born in Ireland.
Adam [3] ______ you start school there?
Rachel No, I [4] ______ . I [5] ______ school here, in London. We moved here ten years [6] ______ .
Adam Why did [7] ______ move to London?
Rachel We [8] ______ because my dad got a new job.
Adam [9] ______ you miss your friends in Ireland [10] ______ you moved?
Rachel Yes, I [11] ______ . I [12] ______ them a lot. But it was a long time ago. I'm okay now.

Your Turn

8 Complete the questions and write true answers.

1 Where *were you born?* (you / born)
I was born in ______
2 When ______ (you / start) school?
______
3 How old ______ (be / you) then?
______
4 Where ______ (you / live) then?
______
5 When ______ (you / have) your first English lesson?
______
6 ______ (your class / use) *Challenges* last year?
______

9 Complete the questions and answers about Joss Stone.

Joss Stone, soul singer

Q When [1] *was she born* ?
A She was born [2] ______ 1987.
Q [3] ______ grow up?
A She [4] ______ in Devon, England.
Q [5] ______ she a good student?
A No, she [6] ______ . She wasn't really into school work!
Q Why [7] ______ start singing soul music?
A She [8] ______ singing soul music because she heard Aretha Franklin.
Q [9] ______ did she make her first album?
A She [10] ______ her first album when she [11] ______ sixteen.

10 Read the notes and the text about Jamie Bell. Find and correct five mistakes in the text.

born: 1986, Billingham (England)
first dancing class: 1992 (age 6)
made film *Billy Elliot*: 2000 (age 14)
won a 'British Oscar' (a Bafta): 2001 (age 15)
left school, moved to London: 2002 (age 16)
played part of Jimmy in Peter Jackson's film *King Kong*: 2005 (age 19)

Jamie Bell was born in 1988 in an English town called Billingham. He took his first dancing class when he was seven. When he was fourteen, he made the film Billy Elliot, and in 2001 he won an Oscar. Then, in 2002, Jamie left school and moved to the USA. When he was nineteen he played the part of King Kong in Peter Jackson's film.

1 *He wasn't born in 1988. He was born in 1986.*
2 ______
3 ______
4 ______
5 ______

1 **Read the text. Choose the correct answer.**

Owen wrote the text for his *homework/a competition*.

Favourite Animations

What's your favourite animated film?

Is it *Shrek*, or perhaps *Toy Story*, or *The Fantastic Mr Fox*? Write and tell us! There's a £10 prize for the best letter.

I think the best animated films are *Toy Story 1, 2* and *3*. The films are CGI (computer generated imagery) and the pictures are fantastic. They made the first one in 1995. That was before I was born!

Toy Story 2 was the first film I saw at the cinema. My parents took my older sister for her sixth birthday and I went too. I was very young but I loved it. For my next birthday, my grandparents gave me both films on DVD and I watched them all the time.

The films are about a boy called Andy and his toys. In the first film, he is about seven years old and in the second he is a bit older. His toys, including Woody and Buzz Lightyear, are great characters. They are the heroes but each film has a villain. These bad characters always plan to harm the toys but after lots of exciting, funny and frightening events, the toys always win.

In 2010, eleven years after *Toy Story 2*, there was the third and final film. This I time went with my friends, not my family. We were all fourteen and we loved it! Like us, Andy was older – he's about eighteen in the film – so it was time to say goodbye to his toys.

Owen, Bolton

Vocabulary

2 **Read the clues and find the words in the text.**

1 people in a film, play or book: *c h a r a c t e r s*
2 brave or good people: h _ _ _ _ _
3 to do something bad to a person: h _ _ _
4 the bad person in a film, play or book: v _ _ _ _ _ _ _
5 things that happen: e _ _ _ _ _
6 the last thing: f _ _ _ _

Reading

3 **Complete the sentences about the text in Exercise 1. Choose a), b) or c).**

1 Owen's letter is mainly about …
  (a) the *Toy Story* films.
  b) his DVD collection.
  c) going to the cinema.

2 Owen …
  a) only likes *Toy Story* films.
  b) sometimes goes to the cinema.
  c) doesn't like films with real actors.

3 Owen saw *Toy Story 1* …
  a) at the cinema.
  b) on TV.
  c) at home.

4 Owen saw ________ of the films at the cinema.
  a) one
  b) two
  c) three

5 Andy, the boy in the film, …
  a) has got two toys.
  b) hasn't got any friends.
  c) has got some toys.

6 Andy is …
  a) a child in all the films.
  b) the same age as Owen.
  c) a teenager in the last film.

4 Read about another animated film and complete the text. Choose a), b) or c).

Snow White and The Seven Dwarves is
1 ___b___ animated film. They made it
2 ________ 1937. It was the first colour animation
3 ________ .

In the story, the 4 ________ the queen. The queen hates Snow White because she is young and beautiful. Snow White runs away from the palace and lives with 5 ________ dwarves. They look 6 ________ Snow White but the queen finds her and gives her a bad apple. Snow White is very ill 7 ________ a prince kisses her and she wakes up.

There are twenty-five 8 ________ in the film including *Love's First Kiss* 9 ________ *It's a Girl*. But the 10 ________ famous song is *Heigh Ho* – the dwarves sing it when they go to work.

1	**a)** the	(**b**) an	**c)** my
2	**a)** in	**b)** on	**c)** to
3	**a)** actor	**b)** story	**c)** film
4	**a)** villain	**b)** villains	**c)** villain's
5	**a)** some	**b)** any	**c)** a
6	**a)** before	**b)** to	**c)** after
7	**a)** because	**b)** but	**c)** and
8	**a)** song	**b)** songs	**c)** song's
9	**a)** but	**b)** because	**c)** and
10	**a)** more	**b)** less	**c)** most

5 Complete the sentences. Use the verbs in the box.

Word Builder

got had ~~looked after~~ made travelled wrote

1 I *looked after* our neighbour's dog at the weekend.
2 Mr and Mrs Dawson ____________ a baby in April.
3 They ____________ friends with some people on the beach.
4 My aunt ____________ married to a man from Canada.
5 Owen ____________ a letter about his favourite animated films.
6 They ____________ round France on bikes.

6 Write sentences in the Past Simple.

Sentence Builder

1 We / decide / go / camping
We decided to go camping.

2 I / try / phone / you yesterday / three times
____

3 When / they / decide / go / to England / ?
____

4 I / not / want / go / out last night
____

5 When / you / start / study / English / ?
____

9 Communication

14 **1 Read, listen and find these people. Write their names under the photo.**

Charlie	Charlie's girlfriend	grandfather	grandmother	Julia	Steve

1 Sarah
2 Ron
3 ______
4 ______
5 Jane
6 ______
7 ______
8 ______
9 Catherine
10 ______
11 David

May Look at this picture of my grandparents when they got married. It's very funny.
Dan Who's the man with the amazing hair?
May That's my Great Uncle Charlie. The girl with the long hair was his girlfriend I think.
Dan What about the girl in the short skirt?
May Do you mean the girl in the big shoes?
Dan Yes, who is she?
May That's my Great Aunt Julia. She was really into fashion then! And the boy with the long hair in a ponytail is her husband now. My Uncle Steve.

2 **Complete these sentences about the people in Exercise 1. Use *in* or *with* and the words in the box.**

Sentence Builder

the big hat the flowers the black and white dress ~~no hair~~ the short trousers

1 Uncle Ron is the man *with no hair* .
2 The little boy ________ is Uncle David.
3 The girl ________ is Aunt Jane.
4 Great Aunt Catherine is the woman ________ .
5 Aunt Sarah is the woman ________ .

Key Expressions: Describing photos

3 **Complete the sentences about the photo in Exercise 1. Use *at*, *in* or *on* and the words in the box.**

the back the front the left ~~the middle~~ the right

1 Mary's grandparents are *in the middle* of the picture.
2 Great Aunt Catherine is ________ .
3 Uncle David is ________ .
4 Aunt Sarah is ________ .
5 Aunt Jane is ________ .

Listening

15 **4** **Listen to a programme about Angelina Jolie. Complete the information.**

ANGELINA JOLIE

born:	1 *4th June 1975*
born in:	2 ________
age when her dad won an OSCAR:	3 ________
age when she acted in her first film:	4 ________
age when she started acting lessons:	5 ________
year she starred in the first Lara Croft film:	6 ________
how many children she's got:	7 ________

16 **5** **Listen again and write down an interesting fact about Angelina Jolie.**

____
____

17 **6** **Listen to May talking to her grandmother. Complete the sentences. Choose a), b) or c).**

1 May is …
 (a) 14.
 b) 15.
 c) 16.
2 May's grandmother liked …
 a) Spam.
 b) The Beatles.
 c) The Rolling Stones.
3 The Beatles concert was in …
 a) London.
 b) Oxford.
 c) Birmingham.
4 When she went to the concert, she lived in …
 a) London.
 b) Oxford.
 c) Birmingham.
5 She's got …
 a) the programme.
 b) the programme and some magazines.
 c) some magazines and pictures.
6 She thinks the box is …
 a) on a shelf.
 b) in a cupboard.
 c) at Aunt Julia's house.

Reading Corner 2

1 **Read the text quickly. Choose the best title (1–3).**

1 The Best Band
2 Number One Song Writers
3 A Famous Musician

John Lennon was born in 1940 in Liverpool, England. When John was five, his father left the family so he went to live with his Aunt Mimi and Uncle George. John saw his mother sometimes and she taught him to play the banjo. When he was a teenager, Aunt Mimi bought him a guitar. Sadly, the year after John Lennon left high school, his mother died in a car accident outside Aunt Mimi's house.

Soon after his mother died, John made friends with Paul McCartney. They both played the guitar and they started to write songs together. They decided to start a band with another guitarist and a drummer and The Beatles were born.

In the 1960s, The Beatles were the most famous band in the world. Young people copied their clothes and hairstyles to look like them. John and Paul wrote the band's songs and they sold millions of records. The Beatles also starred in some very successful movies.

In 1970 the band split up and John moved to the United States with his second wife, Yoko Ono. They became peace activists because they wanted to stop wars.

Then, in 1980, a man called Mark Chapman murdered John Lennon outside his apartment in New York. His death shocked millions of people all over the world.

2 **Find the Past Simple form of the verbs (1–5) in the text. Match them with the correct meanings (a–d).**

	verb		**meaning**
1	die	**a)**	do the same as another person
2	copy	**b)**	make people surprised and unhappy
3	split up	**c)**	stop living
4	murder	**d)**	stop being together
5	shock	**e)**	kill a person

3 **Complete the sentences with the Past Simple form of the verbs in Exercise 2.**

1 The bad news *shocked* all of us.
2 The teacher ________ Rod and Sam because they talked a lot.
3 We've got the same answers. You ________ my work!
4 The man ________ two people before the police caught him.
5 Our dog ________ because she was very old and ill.

4 **Complete the sentences about the text in Exercise 1. Choose a), b) or c).**

1 John Lennon's childhood was difficult because …
   a) he got bad marks at school.
   (b)) he didn't live with his mother and father.
   c) he couldn't play an instrument.
2 There were ________ musicians in The Beatles.
   a) two
   b) three
   c) four
3 The Beatles became famous …
   a) when John played the banjo.
   b) after John's mother died.
   c) before John's dad went away.
4 The Beatles were most successful …
   a) in the 1960s.
   b) after people copied their hair and clothes.
   c) when they sang other people's songs.
5 John Lennon got married to …
   a) one woman.
   b) two women.
   c) three women.
6 In the 1970s, John Lennon …
   a) made friends with Mark Chapman.
   b) played in another rock band.
   c) went to live in the United States.

5 **The words in the box are about music. Find them in the text. Then complete the summary about John Lennon.**

band drummer guitar guitarist ~~played~~ songs

John Lennon was a famous musician. When he was young, he [1] *played* the banjo. He learned the [2] ________ when he was older. When he met another [3] ________, Paul McCartney, they started to write [4] ________ together. Soon after, they started a [5] ________ called The Beatles. The band had three guitarists and a [6] ________ .

6 **Find and write the American English words.**

British English	**American English**
secondary school	
film	
flat	

Language Check 3

Vocabulary

1 Write the dates in two ways.

1st February 2007	*The first of February two thousand and seven*
1 ______	The thirteenth of July nineteen ninety-five
22nd January 1860	2 ______
3 ______	The twenty-fourth of August two thousand and six
3rd November 2010	4 ______
5 ______	The thirtieth of October nineteen ninety-eight
12th December 2012	6 ______

☐ / 6

2 Complete the words in the sentences.

I s*a* *w* my teacher in town yesterday.

1 Last night, I w_ _ _ _ a letter to my grandparents.
2 Sam m_ _ _ friends with Mark at the party last weekend.
3 Our aunt visited us last Saturday so my mum m_ _ _ a special meal.
4 My older brother l_ _ _ home when he went to university.
5 At Henry's party we all h_ _ burgers and ice cream.
6 People w_ _ _ jeans in the nineteenth century.
7 In 2010 my family w_ _ _ to The Beatles museum in Liverpool.
8 She g_ _ a skateboard for her last birthday.
9 Our neighbours l_ _ _ _ _ a_ _ _ _ our cat when we were on holiday.

☐ / 9

Grammar

3 Find the odd one out.

	talked	*got*	*(write)*	*took*
1	score	lived	start	be
2	liked	won	studied	play
3	want	work	went	walk
4	meet	had	made	was
5	take	have	finish	spent

☐ / 5

4 Complete the questions and answers.

'What time did you go to bed last night?' (go)
'I went to bed at 10.' (go)

1 'What ______ on TV last night?' (watch)
'I ______ *The Simpsons*.' (watch)
2 'Where ______ at 8 o'clock this morning?' (be)
'I ______ in bed.' (be)
3 'What ______ for lunch today?' (have)
'We ______ cheese sandwiches.' (have)
4 '______ the dishes yesterday?' (do)
'(yes) ______ '
5 '______ your bed this morning?' (make)
'(no) ______ .'

☐ / 10

Key Expressions

5 Complete the description of a family photo. Use the words in the box.

at back middle ~~of~~ on right

This is a photo [1] *of* me when I was eight years old. I'm [2] ______ the front with my dog. That's my grandmother in the [3] ______ . The man on the [4] ______ is my uncle. The woman [5] ______ the left is his girlfriend. The man at the [6] ______ is my grandfather.

☐ / 5

What's your score?

Module 3

☐ Vocabulary
☐ Grammar
☐ Key Expressions
☐ / 35

This is easy.
I need more practice.
This is difficult.

Module 4 Mysteries

Get Ready

Vocabulary: Creatures

1 Match the creatures (1–10) with the descriptions (a–j).

1 ghost	i	**a)** It comes from a strange planet.
2 mermaid		**b)** He's very short and he's got very big feet.
3 fairy		**c)** It lives in the sea, and it's horrible.
4 yeti		**d)** He sleeps in the day and he's got big teeth.
5 werewolf		**e)** She wears a big, black hat, and she can fly.
6 alien		**f)** It's big, white and hairy, and it lives in snowy places.
7 vampire		**g)** It's like a very big, very horrible dog.
8 witch		**h)** A small person with wings and magic powers.
9 hobbit		**i)** You can't always see it!
10 sea monster		**j)** She's got a fish's tail.

Listening

18 **2 Sandy is telling a ghost story. Listen and choose the correct words.**

1. Sandy was (*seven*)/*fourteen* when the story happened.
2. Sandy and her parents stayed in *one room/two rooms*.
3. The old woman appeared *before/after* Sandy went to bed.
4. The old woman *spoke/didn't speak*.
5. Sandy's parents *saw/didn't see* the ghost.
6. The photos were on the walls *upstairs/downstairs*.
7. The photos showed *the same/a different* building.
8. She *is/isn't* sure she saw the ghost in the photo.
9. When she saw the photo, she felt *better/worse*.
10. She *is/isn't* scared now.

Your Turn

3 Read the question and complete the answer. Use your own ideas.

Do you like ghost stories? Why/Why not?
I *like/don't like* ghost stories because

10 Vocabulary and Grammar

Vocabulary: Senses

1 Write the verbs under the correct pictures.

hear see smell taste touch

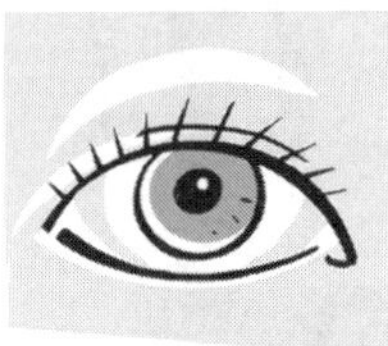

1 *see*

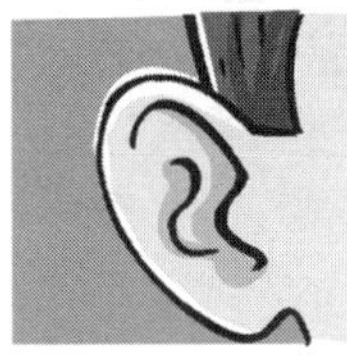

2 ________

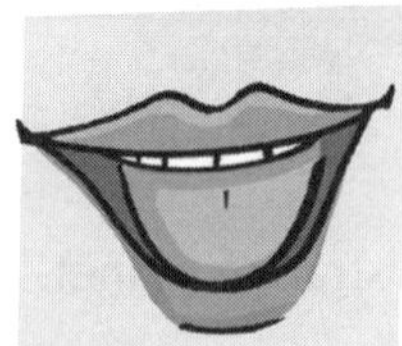

3 ________

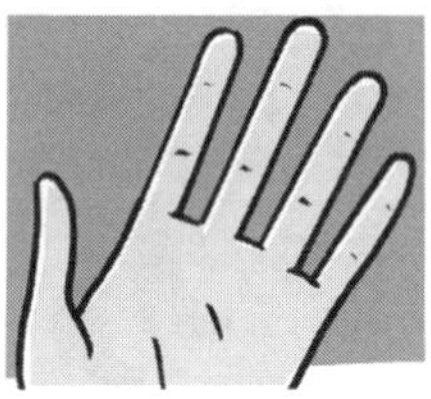

4 ________

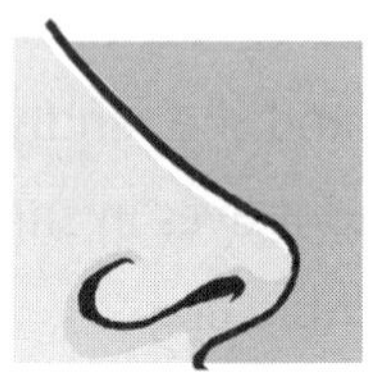

5 ________

2 Complete the sentences. Use the verbs in Exercise 1.

1 Our dinner's in the cooker. I can *smell* it!
2 The music isn't very loud. I can't ________ it.
3 Don't ________ the things in the museum, please.
4 Please turn on the lights – I can't ________ .
5 Try this drink. Can you ________ the oranges?

Grammar: Past Continuous

➤ Grammar Reference, page 103

☆ **3 Match the questions (1–6) and the answers (a–f).**

1 What were they doing at six o'clock last night? *c*
2 I saw you and Jo at the bus stop yesterday. Where were you going? ☐
3 Why wasn't Sara at the party? ☐
4 Why were you wearing your best clothes yesterday? ☐
5 We saw you in town on Saturday. Were you buying new clothes? ☐
6 Why didn't you phone last night? ☐

a We were going to the cinema.
b She was looking after her baby sister.
c They were watching *The Simpsons*.
d My mobile wasn't working. Sorry.
e I was going to a party.
f No, I wasn't.

☆☆ **4 Complete the dialogues with the verbs in the Past Continuous.**

1
What *were you doing* (you / do) at one o'clock last night?
I *was finishing* (finish) my maths homework.

2
What time did John phone?
Eight o'clock. He ________ (come) back from London on the train.

3
I saw you in the geography lesson. Your eyes were closed!
Yes, but I ________ (not / sleep). I ________ (think).

4
Did you miss the school trip today?
No. I got to school late, but they ________ (wait) for me.

5
What did I say? ________ (you / listen) to me?
No, I ________ . Sorry.

Grammar: Past Simple and Past Continuous

➤ Grammar Reference, page 104

☆ **5 Choose the correct form of the verbs.**

1 We *were having*/*had* lunch when a strange thing *was happening/happened*.
2 I *was looking/looked* for my mobile when I *was finding/found* £5 in my pocket!
3 When I *was seeing/saw* John at the party, he *was dancing/danced*.
4 They *were watching/watched* a film when they *were hearing/heard* an explosion.
5 I *wasn't wearing/didn't wear* a coat when I *was going/went* out this morning.
6 When my mum *were meeting/met* my dad, they *were studying/studied* at the same university.

☆☆ **6 Complete the sentences with the verbs in the Past Simple or the Past Continuous.**

1 He *was running* (run) home when his mobile ________ (fall) out of his bag.
2 When Harry ________ (phone) me, he ________ (wait) for a bus.
3 I ________ (see) your mum in town yesterday. She ________ (look) for your birthday present!
4 They ________ (play) very loud music, so the neighbours ________ (call) the police.
5 When I ________ (find) my homework, the dog ________ (eat) it.
6 She ________ (carry) three bags when one of them ________ (break).

☆☆☆ **7 Write about the pictures. Use the Past Continuous, the Past Simple and *when*.**

1 I / swim / sea / see / shark
I was swimming in the sea when I saw a big shark.

2 Jack / cycle / dog / run / across the road
____

3 Janice / travel / to London / meet / David Beckham
____

4 My friends / carry / the shopping / drop / some eggs
____

5 I / sleep / hear / strange sound
____

6 What / you / find / walk / on the beach / ?
____

11 Skills

Vocabulary: Adjectives

1 **Write the opposites of these adjectives. Use the words in the box.**

dangerous dark dirty ~~enormous~~ horrible huge long scary strange

1 small *enormous* or ________
2 short ________
3 safe ________
4 clean ________
5 light ________
6 nice ________ or ________
7 normal ________

Reading

2 **Complete the text. Choose a), b) or c).**

Where do animals like leopards live? Africa? Asia? Well, yes, but [1] *c* are some in Britain, too – and not just in zoos! Every year, more and more people [2]____ strange creatures in the British countryside. They usually describe animals [3]____ small ears and long tails – like giant cats. These creatures disappear quickly, and there aren't [4]____ good photographs, but police believe they are really there. They [5]____ attack people, but when they [6]____ hungry they sometimes attack sheep. [7]____ did they get there? Here's one idea: in the 1970s, many circuses stopped using 'big cats' in [8]____ shows. The animals didn't [9]____ homes anymore. Some owners wanted [10]____ their huge pets, so they took them into the countryside. Now, [11]____ thirty or forty years, the number of 'big cats' in the British countryside is growing.

circus

	a)	b)	c)
1	a) they	b) their	c) there
2	a) see	b) saw	c) sees
3	a) and	b) in	c) with
4	a) some	b) any	c) a
5	a) aren't	b) don't	c) doesn't
6	a) be	b) have	c) get
7	a) Where	b) How many	c) How
8	a) there	b) their	c) they're
9	a) have	b) having	c) had
10	a) saving	b) save	c) to save
11	a) after	b) later	c) during

3 **Complete the sentences. Use the correct form of *get* and the adjectives in the box.**

Word Builder

angry cold hungry nervous

1 The animal was shy. When it saw us it *got nervous* and disappeared.
2 The leopard ________ so it killed a sheep.
3 Some animals sleep all winter. They go to sleep when it ________ .
4 A fox attacked some chickens. The farmer ________ very ________ .

4 **Complete the stories. Write one word in each gap.**

a) Iain Taylor is a runner. One day he [1] *was* running in a race across the Scottish countryside [2]________ he saw a very large black cat in the trees. He ran very fast and won the race! Before that race, he [3]________ believe stories about scary animals in the forest. Now, he thinks they are true!

b) Mary O'Connor, a school cleaner in Scotland, was walking to work [4]________ 6 o'clock in the morning when she saw [5]________ enormous black creature in [6]________ of her. She turned [7]________ ran down the street. Police believe [8]________ saw a leopard.

c) At 2.30 in the morning, some friends [9]________ driving home from a party in [10]________ north of England. They saw [11]________ animal's eyes in the car's lights, so they drove slowly. Then they saw the animal – it [12]________ an enormous cat. It [13]________ small ears and a long tail and it was black or brown.

5 **Complete the sentences. Use the possessive pronouns in the box.**

Sentence Builder

hers ~~his~~ mine ours theirs yours

1 Iain Taylor is a runner. Those trainers are *his* .
2 Mrs O'Connor hasn't got a camera so the photos aren't ________ .
3 Mr and Mrs Lennox weren't in a taxi. The car was ________ .
4 We've got a cat but the enormous black creature in the garden isn't ________ !
5 The pretty white cat is ________ . I got it for my birthday.
6 The camera on the ground is ________ . You dropped it when you ran away from the big cat.

6 **Match the pictures (1–4) and the stories (a–c) in Exercise 3. There is one extra picture.**

1 ☐

2 ☐

3 ☐

4 ☐

7 **Write a story about the extra picture in Exercise 6.**

John and Mandy were going home after a party. It was dark and ________________

12 Communication

Vocabulary

1 Choose the correct words.

1 We went to the party *at/(in)/on* eighteenth-century clothes.
2 Did you hear the story *about/on/to* the monster?
3 In the film, the man fell *at/in/to* love with an alien.
4 The child looked *at/in/on* us and then she disappeared!
5 I got *at/on/to* the haunted house but I was very scared so I didn't go in.
6 *At/In/On* 2009, people in the east of England saw strange lights in the sky.

2 Complete the dialogue with the words in the box.

after end honestly ~~like~~ one suddenly then when

A My friend and I saw an alien last year.
B Really? What happened?
A Well, it started [1] *like* this. [2]________ day, we were walking home [3]________ school. [4]________ , we heard a loud noise and a strange creature appeared!
B No!
A [5]________ ! It was very scary. It was coming towards us [6]________ my friend shouted, 'Go away!'. [7]________ it disappeared!
B Where did it go?
A I don't know. We waited 30 minutes but in the [8]________ we went home.

Listening

19 **3 Jenny and Harry are talking about films. Listen and choose the correct answer.**

1 What does Jenny think of horror films?
a) She loves them. **(b)** She hates them. **c)** They're okay.
2 Who watched *Ghost Story*?
a) Harry **b)** Harry and Jenny **c)** Harry, Jenny and Jenny's sister
3 What kind of films does Jenny like?
a) scary **b)** exciting **c)** true
4 Did Harry watch *Close Encounters*?
a) Yes, he did. **b)** He saw part of it. **c)** No, he didn't.
5 Why does Harry dislike *Close Encounters*?
a) It's about aliens. **b)** It's about a little boy. **c)** It's old.
6 What does Harry think of horror films?
a) They're scary and funny. **b)** They're scary and stupid. **c)** They're stupid and funny.

20 **4 Listen to five short conversations. Choose the correct answers.**

1 What did Harry do last night?

a) ☐

b) ☐

c) ☑

2 What happened at the end of the film?

a) ☐

b) ☐

c) ☐

3 What did Jenny do?

a) ☐

b) ☐

c) ☐

4 What did she do at the Internet café?

a) ☐

b) ☐

c) ☐

5 What did Jenny watch last night?

a) ☐

b) ☐

c) ☐

Writing Challenge 2

1 **Read this student's story. Find the missing sentences (a–e) for each gap.**

a) In the end Katie's dad thought it was probably a joke.
b) Last year, I went on holiday with my friend Katie's family.
c) On the second day, we had a strange adventure.
d) Suddenly, Katie's dad stopped the car.
e) Then it suddenly flew up into the sky and disappeared.

A Strange Adventure

1 ______b______ . We stayed in a little house in the middle of the countryside. It was a great holiday.

2 ____________ . We were driving home from the beach. It was getting dark and we were all singing stupid songs.

3 ____________ . When we looked out of the window we saw a strange silver thing in the road in front of us. It was big and round and it was moving slowly up and down. We were very surprised and scared. Katie's dad decided to get out of the car. We all shouted 'stop!' but he didn't listen. He was opening the car door when the silver thing started to make a noise. 4 ____________ .

We went back to the house and phoned the police. They didn't believe us.

5 ____________ . I don't agree – I think it was a UFO.

2 **Write a story about UFOs or aliens. Write three paragraphs.**

paragraph 1 when? where? who?	____________
paragraph 2 What happened? How did people feel?	____________
paragraph 3 What happened in the end?	____________

Understanding Grammar: *some, any, a lot of, no*

➤ Grammar Reference, page 105

☆ **1 Put the nouns in the box in the correct columns.**

book ~~creature~~ elephant film ~~food~~
life boat music biscuit shark
violence water weather weight wood

Countable nouns	Uncountable nouns
creature	*food*

☆ **2 Read the sentences about the *Mary Celeste*. Choose the correct words.**

1 There weren't (*any*)/*some* sailors on the ship.
2 There were *any/no* instruments of navigation.
3 Did they find *any/some* fresh water on the ship?
4 They found *some/any* food.
5 Five hundred! That's *a lot of/no* barrels.
6 The ship was very tidy and there was *no/any* damage.
7 Was there *any/no* bad weather?

☆ **3 Complete the short conversations. Use *some*, *any*, *a lot of* or *no*.**

1 **A** I liked the film. There were [1] *a lot of* hobbits – they are my favourite fantasy creatures – and there was no violence.
B I didn't like it. It wasn't exciting or scary. There were [2] ______ werewolves or zombies.

2 **A** Do you know [3] ______ mystery stories?
B Yes, I know [4] ______ ghost stories. My dad told me hundreds when I was younger.

3 **A** Have you got [5] ______ DVDs about UFOs?
B No, I haven't. But I've got [6] ______ about vampires. There are three or four on the bookshelf.

4 **A** Did you get *The Lord of the Rings* when you went to the library?
B No, I didn't. There weren't [7] ______ fantasy books.

☆☆☆ **4 Use the words to write about the pictures. There may be several possible answers.**

A

1 fantasy books *There are no/There aren't any fantasy books.*
2 history books *There are a lot of history books.*
3 English books *There are some English books.*

B

1 sailors ______
2 food ______
3 water ______

C

1 spaceships ______
2 aliens ______
3 people ______

Language Check 4

Vocabulary

1 Find six creatures.

(hobbit)vampireghostwitchalienfairyzombie

hobbit

1 ______ 4 ______
2 ______ 5 ______
3 ______ 6 ______

☐ / 6

2 Choose the correct words.

Where's my book? I can't taste/(see) it.

1 Listen! Can you *hear/see* music?
2 There is coffee in this cake. Can you *touch/taste* it?
3 Oh no! I can *smell/hear* smoke.
4 'What's that green thing in the sky?' – 'Where? I can't *hear/see* it.'
5 Don't *touch/hear* this plate. It's hot.

☐ / 5

3 Find the odd one out.

	dangerous	*horrible*	*(long)*	*scary*
1	angry	round	nervous	scared
2	enormous	huge	big	dirty
3	dark	hungry	tired	angry
4	scary	cold	horrible	strange

☐ / 4

Grammar

4 Put the verbs in the Past Simple or the Past Continuous.

We were walking (walk) home when we saw (see) a fire.

1 I ______ (sleep) when the phone ______ (ring).
2 It ______ (get) dark when the accident ______ (happen).
3 Where ______ (you / go) when I ______ (see) you at the station?
4 We ______ (watch) a football match when the rain ______ (start).
5 Sorry. ______ (you / ask a question)? I ______ (not / listen).

☐ / 10

5 Complete the sentences with *some*, *any*, *a lot of* or *no*.

Did you get any books from the library?

1 He takes ______ fruit to school every day.
2 Were ______ students late for the lesson?
3 She couldn't go out for a week so she watched ______ DVDs. She watched four every day!
4 We didn't have ______ bread for sandwiches.
5 I went to school in the holiday and there were ______ students. It was very strange.

☐ / 5

Key Expressions

6 Choose the correct words.

We were watching TV *(one day)/then*. I think it was *The Simpsons*. [1] *Suddenly/When* Jack jumped up [2] *and/then* said, 'I can smell smoke!' [3] *After/When* about a minute we saw smoke, too. It was coming from the TV. [4] *When/Then* the fire started, [5] *so/suddenly* we ran out of the room and called for help.

☐ / 5

What's your score?

Module 4

☐ Vocabulary
☐ Grammar
☐ Key Expressions
☐ / 35

This is easy.
I need more practice.
This is difficult.

Module 5 Performers

Get Ready

Vocabulary: Performers

1 Read the clues and find the people in the word square.

1 He finds rabbits in his hat! *magician*
2 She never moves! ______
3 He dances on ice. ______
4 She does amazing exercises. ______
5 He throws and catches. ______
6 He's got a red nose and he's funny. ______
7 She plays music. ______
8 She tells stories. ______
9 He acts. ______
10 She acts, too! ______

B	F	J	M	A	G	I	C	I	A	N	M
H	N	G	L	C	A	C	T	R	E	S	S
U	C	L	C	T	G	Y	P	G	M	R	T
M	R	L	N	O	S	G	Y	G	U	Y	O
A	J	A	O	R	M	L	L	J	S	C	R
N	U	S	T	W	B	E	L	M	I	L	Y
S	G	T	G	H	N	R	D	E	C	S	T
T	G	Y	M	N	A	S	T	I	I	T	E
A	L	P	W	D	G	U	O	A	A	C	L
T	E	S	L	K	O	R	R	T	N	N	L
U	R	I	C	E	S	K	A	T	E	R	E
E	S	K	T	O	R	D	A	N	C	E	R

2 Find two other performers in the word square.

c______
d______

Listening

21 **3 What are their jobs? Listen to the conversations and complete the sentences. Use words from Exercise 1.**

1 Jonathan's *an actor* ______ .
2 Emma's ______ .
3 Steve's ______ .
4 Marion's ______ .

13 Vocabulary and Grammar

Vocabulary

1 Complete the dialogue. Use the verbs in the box.

do earn go (x 2) have spend ~~star~~ work

A Are you a child actor?
B Yes, I am. I [1] *star* in three films every year. I don't [2] ________ to school – I [3] ________ private teachers.
A Do you have to [4] ________ long hours?
B No, I don't. There is a special law for child actors. I work short hours and I don't [5] ________ dangerous activities.
A Do you [6] ________ a lot of money?
B Yes, I do. But it has to [7] ________ into a bank account. I can [8] ________ the money when I'm eighteen.
A That's sounds cool!

Grammar: *can, can't, have to, not have to*

► Grammar Reference, page 106

☆ **2 Choose the correct words.**

1. Actors *don't have to* (circled) / *can't* be good-looking.
2. Teachers *have to/don't have to* wear uniforms.
3. Ice skaters *can/can't* wear trainers when they skate.
4. Footballers *can/have to* practise.
5. Pop singers *have to/don't have to* play the guitar.
6. Dancers *don't have to/can't* be fat.
7. Musicians *don't have to/can't* be singers.
8. Singers *can/have to* have good voices.

☆☆ **3 Correct the sentences.**

1. Dancers don't have to practise every day.
   Dancers have to practise every day.
2. Actors can be shy.
   ____
3. Musicians have to wear make-up.
   ____
4. Comedians have to be good-looking.
   ____
5. Teachers can't tell jokes.
   ____

☆☆☆ **4 Complete the sentences. Use the correct form of *can* or *have to* and the words in brackets.**

1. My dad usually wears casual clothes – *he doesn't have to wear* (he / wear) a suit.
2. Are you going out tonight, or ________ (you / study)?
3. There's no school on Sundays so ________ (we / get up) early – ________ (we / stay) in bed!
4. Jen is a dancer so ________ (she / practise) every day, and ________ (she / eat) chocolate and sweets.
5. ________ (boys / have) long hair at your school, or ________ (they / keep) their hair short?
6. ________ (John / walk) to school because his mum drives him.

Your Turn

☆☆☆ **5 Write about the best or the worst school in the world. Use the correct form of *can* or *have to*. Use the words in the box or your own ideas.**

do clothes computers hair homework lessons parents subjects teachers TV

____
____
____
____
____
____

☆ **6 Read the rules for an unusual dance school. Are the sentences true (T) or false (F)?**

STAGELIGHT

SCHOOL of STREET DANCE

Saturday morning classes

There is no uniform but there are some simple rules:

- Please wear comfortable clothes and trainers. Our shop sells STAGELIGHT T-shirts, trousers and jackets, but your own clothes are fine.
- Do NOT wear boots.
- Do NOT wear jeans or tight trousers.
- Do NOT wear jewellery.
- Remember, NO food or drink in the practice rooms … and NO chewing gum. The snack bar is open during break.
- Please turn off mobiles when you come into school.

1 Students don't have to wear uniform. *T*
2 They have to wear clothes from the school's shop. ☐
3 They can't wear boots. ☐
4 They don't have to wear trainers. ☐
5 They can buy food at break. ☐
6 They can use mobiles in school. ☐

☆☆ **7 Complete the sentences with the correct form of *can* or *have to*.**

Students [1] *have to* wear comfortable clothes. They [2] ________ wear their own clothes or clothes from the school shop. They [3] ________ wear jeans or jewellery. They [4] ________ leave their mobiles at home but they [5] ________ turn them off.

☆☆☆ **8 Complete the dialogue with the correct form of *can* or *have to*.**

A What are your street dance classes like?
B Oh, great! I really enjoy them.
A [1] *Do you have to* (you) go every Saturday?
B Yes, but only in the mornings – we [2] ____________ be there all day!
A [3] ____________ (you) wear special clothes, or [4] ____________ (you) wear your own clothes?
B Well, we [5] ____________ wear jeans – we [6] ____________ wear loose clothes. The school shop sells special T-shirts and things, but we [7] ____________ wear them.

14 Skills

Vocabulary

1 Match the words (1–8) and the pictures (a–h).

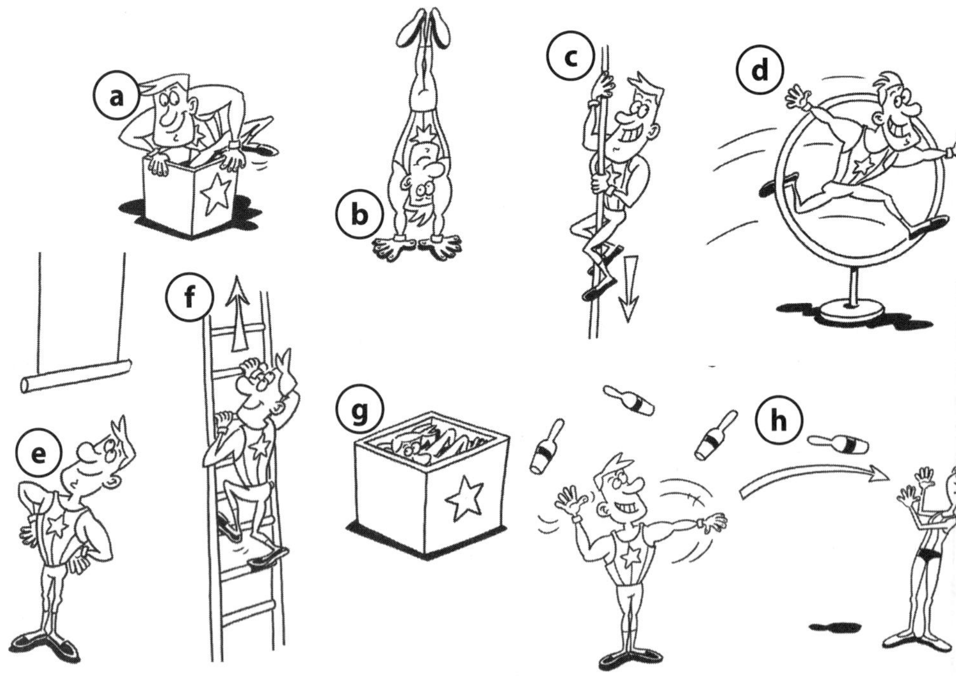

1 down *c*
2 inside
3 into
4 upside down
5 through
6 to
7 up
8 below

2 Choose the correct words.

We went [1]*to/in* the circus last night. It was fantastic.
The trapeze artists performed first. They climbed [2]*through/up* really high and they were amazing. They flew [3]*through/inside* the air like birds. There wasn't a net [4]*below/down* them!
The contortionist was my favourite. He climbed [5]*to/into* a very small box and closed it. Then a clown decided to sit [6]*down/on*. He sat [7]*to/on* the box, of course. The contortionist was [8]*inside/into* it. He shouted and made a noise but the clown didn't move. It was very funny.

3 Read the email in Exercise 2 again. Choose the correct picture.

a ☐

b ☐

4 Complete the sentences with *down, into, on* or *together.*

Word Builder

1 A juggler got ___*on*___ a bike and juggled six balls.
2 The contortionist got ________ the box, and then climbed out again.
3 The trapeze artists got ________ from the ceiling.
4 The acrobats got ________ and made a human pyramid.
5 A clown got ________ some stilts and did a dance.

5 Complete the sentences with words from A and B.

Sentence Builder

A: getting laughing listening ~~looking~~ talking waiting

B: about at for to together ~~up~~

1 'Why are you *looking up* ?'
'Because I can see a strange plane.'

2 'What are you ____________ ?'
'A bus. It's late.'

3 'What are you ____________ ?'
'My new CD. Sssh!'

4 'What are you ____________ ?'
'A joke. It's really funny.'

5 'What are you ____________ ?'
'We're discussing our homework.'

6 'Why are they ____________ ?'
'I think they're planning a party.'

Reading

6 Read the text and choose a), b) or c).

Fun for all

Covent Garden is one of the most popular parts of London. Tourists and Londoners, adults and kids – they all enjoy the great shops, restaurants and cafés, and, most of all, they love the street performers. At Covent Garden, you can see some of the best street performers in the world. There are jugglers, clowns, magicians, living statues, musicians – the list goes on and on!

Before they can perform there, performers have to pass a test (it doesn't cost anything). The shows are free, and performers don't go round and collect money – but most people throw money into the hat! The performers can keep all the money. Sometimes the audience is small but often there are big crowds, and there's a lot of money at the end of the show.

George is an acrobat. He learnt his skills at circus school and then joined a circus and went on tour round Britain. Now he performs at Covent Garden.

'You have to work hard to get an audience,' he says. 'You tell jokes, sing, dance – then when you have a good crowd you can start the show.'

Chantelle plays the violin in an orchestra, but she prefers Covent Garden!

'The crowds are always great here,' she says, 'And the money's better than my orchestra job!'

1 Covent Garden is …
a) mainly popular with tourists. b) mainly popular with Londoners. (c) popular with everybody.

2 Performers have to …
a) pay before they can perform. b) pass a test and pay. c) pass a test.

3 The people in the audience …
a) decide what to pay. b) don't pay anything. c) all pay the same.

4 George …
a) studies circus skills. b) is touring Britain. c) usually performs in London.

5 He usually …
a) starts his show with a big audience. b) starts his show with no audience. c) tries to get a crowd before he starts a show.

6 Chantelle plays at Covent Garden because …
a) she wants to. b) she hasn't got a job. c) her orchestra plays there.

15 Communication

Vocabulary

1 Complete the dialogue with the words and phrases in the box.

give me his number ~~I bet~~ I don't mind okay not on

A It's amazing! Callum got 95 per cent in the test!
B I know. He was sitting next to me and I only got 80 per cent.
A 1 ___*I bet*___ he looked at your answers.
B 2 ____________ .
A That's 3 ____________ ! I want to ring him! Can you 4 ____________ ?
B It's 5 ____________ . I know I did *my* test without looking.

Key Expressions: Suggestions

2 Complete the dialogue. Write one word in each gap.

A Hi Andy. 1 ___*Would*___ you 2 ____________ to play tennis tomorrow?
B All 3 ____________ . What time?
A What 4 ____________ ten o'clock?
B No, that's too early. Why 5 ____________ we play in the afternoon?
A I can't. I'm busy then.
B Oh, well, ten is okay, then.
A 6 ____________ we meet at the sports centre?
B Yes, great.
A Cool.

3 Complete the dialogues. Choose a), b) or c).

1 Would you like to go to the cinema?
 (a) Yes, great.
 b) Yes, I do.
 c) Yes, quite often.

2 Why don't we watch a DVD?
 a) Thanks a lot.
 b) Not now.
 c) I don't like it.

3 What about a pizza?
 a) It's Italian.
 b) I love them.
 c) Cool!

4 Let's go shopping.
 a) Well, not now.
 b) Okay, bye.
 c) Every Saturday.

5 Let's meet at half past seven.
 a) All right.
 b) Okay, what time?
 c) Yes, I'm sure.

6 Would you like to go out on Saturday afternoon?
 a) Not now.
 b) Yes, I'm quite tired.
 c) That's a good idea.

7 Shall we go to the tennis club?
 a) No. It's fine.
 b) Okay. Cool!
 c) Yes, we do.

8 What about the cinema?
 a) Okay, what time?
 b) Yes, I do.
 c) I'm busy then.

Listening

22 **4 Listen to the conversation. What are their plans for the weekend? Write the correct letter next to each day or time.**

Days/Times

1 Friday evening ___*a*___
2 Saturday morning ______
3 Saturday afternoon ______
4 Saturday evening ______
5 Sunday ______
6 Sunday evening ______

Activities

a) band practice
b) homework
c) orchestra
d) party
e) relaxing
f) shopping
g) swimming
h) watching DVDs

23 **5 Listen and complete the information.**

	ABC1	ABC2
Film:	*Dust*	*Tail Back*
Dates:	1 *13–18 June*	13–18 June
Times:	2 ______	7 ______
	3 ______	8 ______
Tickets Adults:	4 ______	
Students:	5 ______	9 ______
Children:	6 ______	

24 **6 Listen and complete the information.**

Dust is about [1] ___*a murder*___ .
It's a film for everyone over the age of [2] ______ .
It's [3] ______ hours and [4] ______ minutes long.
Tail Back is a [5] ______ film about [6] ______ .
It's [7] ______ hours and [8] ______ minutes long.

Writing

7 Complete the information about a film at your local cinema. You can choose any film.

______ (title) is about ______ .
It's ______ long.
It's a film for ______ .
Tickets cost ______ .

Reading Corner 3

The Visitor

1 **Read the information (a–g) about the film script. Match the questions (1–7) and the information.**

a The Visitor

b **CHARACTERS**

ROSE a middle-aged woman, BEN's mother.

BEN a teenage boy

RICHARD a young man

c *All the scenes take place in three parts of Rose's house: the kitchen, the entrance hall and the living room.*

d **Scene 1. Friday evening**

e *ROSE is washing up in the kitchen. She's singing. The doorbell rings.*

f **ROSE**

g Oh, who's that? Another one of Ben's friend's, I guess.

1 How many people are in the play, and who are they? *b*
2 Where does the story happen? ☐
3 When does it happen? ☐
4 What's the name of the play? ☐
5 Who is speaking? ☐
6 What does he or she say? ☐
7 What happens first? ☐

2 **Read Scene 1. Choose the correct words.**

1 Richard is probably a *friend/stranger.*
2 Johnny is probably Ben's *father/brother.*
3 Rose probably feels *relaxed/worried.*

Scene 1. The bell rings again

BEN Mum! Somebody's at the door!

ROSE Yes, yes, okay, I'm coming.

ROSE goes to the front door and opens it.

RICHARD is standing there. He is wearing a suit and holding some flowers.

RICHARD Hello. I'm so sorry I'm late. I got lost!

ROSE Oh, hello. I'm sorry but …

RICHARD Oh, is dinner late? It's okay, don't worry, I'm not very hungry right now. Here, these are for you. Can I come in?

RICHARD hands the flowers to ROSE and steps into the house.

ROSE Ben! Can you come here, please?

BEN appears. ROSE turns and speaks to him quietly.

ROSE Who's this? Do you know him?

BEN *(quietly)* No, I don't. He's probably one of dad's friends from work.

ROSE Yes, you're probably right. *(to RICHARD)* Come and sit down. Sorry about the mess.

RICHARD Thank you. What a lovely house!

They enter the living room and Richard sits down on the sofa.

ROSE Johnny will be home soon, Mr … Mr … oh, silly me, I don't know your surname!

RICHARD It's Green. But please call me Richard.

ROSE Oh, and I'm Rose, of course. You don't have to call me Mrs Harris!

RICHARD Thank you, Rose. Well it will be nice to see Johnny again after all these years.

ROSE Oh, yes, of course … Can I get you a drink?

RICHARD Yes, thanks …

ROSE goes into the kitchen and makes a phone call.

ROSE Johnny, is that you? Listen, who's this Richard person? ... Green, I think he said Green … Well, he's young, he's wearing a suit … He's sitting on our sofa, and I think he's staying for dinner. Who is he? …

End of Scene 1

3 **At the end of Scene 1, Rose is on the telephone to Johnny. Guess what Johnny is saying. Complete the conversation.**

Rose Johnny, is that you?
Johnny *Yes, hi.* ____________
Rose Listen, who is this Richard person?
Johnny ____________
Rose Green. I think he said Green.
Johnny ____________
Rose Well, he's young, he's wearing a suit …
Johnny ____________
Rose He's sitting on our sofa, and I think he's staying for dinner. Who is he?
Johnny ____________

4 **Read Scene 2 and complete this sentence.**
I think the person at the door is ____________
____________.

Scene 2. Ten minutes later

ROSE enters the living room, carrying three drinks. RICHARD and BEN are chatting.

RICHARD So, you're just like your dad, then, crazy about sport.

ROSE gives a drink to RICHARD and BEN.

ROSE How did you know … I mean, how did you meet Johnny?

RICHARD Oh Rose, what a strange question. You were there! It was a long time ago, I know. Before Ben was born, of course.

ROSE I was there? Oh, yes, of course … Ben, can I have some help in the kitchen, please?

BEN Oh, okay, then.

ROSE Please excuse us for a minute, Richard.

RICHARD Of course. Can I put the TV on?

He switches the TV on.

ROSE Oh, yes, of course.

ROSE and BEN go into the kitchen. ROSE closes the door.

ROSE Ben, is this one of your jokes? Because it isn't very funny.

BEN Mum, I don't know him. I don't know anything about him. I …

The doorbell rings

ROSE Oh dear, what now?

ROSE and BEN go into the entrance hall. RICHARD is opening the door.

RICHARD Hi, come in!

End of Scene 2

5 **Write the next scene as a film script or write a paragraph to complete the story. Use one of these suggestions, or use your own ideas.**

- Richard is an actor. The person at the door is a TV presenter. It's part of a TV show.
- Richard is a criminal.
- Richard is Johnny's friend. It's 1st April.

____

Language Check 5

Vocabulary

1 Answer the questions with the words in the box.

acrobat comedian human statue ice skater magician ~~musician~~ singer storyteller

Who plays an instrument? musician

1 Who is funny? ____________
2 Who has to speak a lot? ____________
3 Who has to be strong? ____________
4 Who has to stand still? ____________
5 Who wears special boots? ____________
6 Who has a good voice? ____________
7 Who can do card tricks? ____________

☐ / 7

2 Complete the sentences with the words in the box.

about at from down for into on to ~~together~~

We got together and collected a lot of money.

1 Don't wait ________ a bus, we can walk.
2 Nobody laughed ________ the teacher's jokes.
3 Don't talk ________ your friends when they're not here.
4 Sid got ________ his motorbike and rode away.
5 A bird got ________ our house and flew all round the kitchen.
6 Do you come ________ Britain, or are you American?
7 Please be quiet and listen ________ me.
8 How do you get ________ from the top of the mountain?

☐ / 8

Grammar

3 Choose the correct words.

Children (can't)/don't have to drive cars.

1 I *can/have to* study. I *can't/don't have to* leave school.
2 Bus drivers *can't/don't have to* be men. They *can/have to* be women, too.
3 You need a student card. Then you *can/have to* get a discount.

☐ / 5

4 Complete the sentences with *can*, *can't*, *have to* or *not have to*.

We're on holiday so we don't have to work.

1 You ________ use your mobile in the library – please go outside.
2 The tickets are free for students, so we ________ pay!
3 Please take that chewing gum outside. You ________ have that in class!
4 My mum works late on Fridays so I ________ cook the dinner.
5 I did my homework yesterday so I ________ relax now!

(2 points for each question) ☐ / 10

Key Expressions

5 Complete the phone call. Write one word in each gap.

A What about the cinema this afternoon?
B No, there's nothing on.
A Okay, [1]________ go cycling.
B It's raining.
A Well, [2]________ don't we go shopping?
B I haven't got any money.
A [3]________ you like [4]________ come and play my new computer game?
B [5]________ right. Cool!

☐ / 5

What's your score?

Module 5

☐ Vocabulary
☐ Grammar
☐ Key Expressions
☐ / 35

This is easy.
I need more practice.
This is difficult.

Get Ready

Vocabulary: Appearance (1)

1 **Write the names under the pictures.**

- **Anne** is very young.
- **Maisie** is a tall, slim teenager.
- **Claire** is a short, young woman.
- **Josh** is a very good-looking man.
- **Rita** is middle-aged.
- **Thomas** is an old man.

1 ____________

2 *Anne*

3 ____________

4 ____________

5 ____________

6 ____________

2 **Look at the pictures again. Complete the sentences with the words in the box.**

curly fat handsome long round ~~short~~ square straight tall thin

1 Maisie's got *short* , brown hair and a ____________ face.
2 Anne is a ____________ baby. She's got a very pretty, ____________ face.
3 Claire's hair is long and ____________ .
4 Josh is very ____________ .
5 Rita's plump and she's got ____________ hair.
6 Thomas is ____________ and ____________ . He's got a very ____________ face.

Listening

25 **3** **Listen and complete the table. Then draw the faces.**

	hair	eyes
 John	*fair* ____________ ____________	____________
 Holly	____________ ____________ ____________	____________ ____________

16 Vocabulary and Grammar

Vocabulary: Appearance (2)

1 Match the phrases.

1	cut/dye/grow your	a)	weight
2	change	b)	in your hair
3	grow a	c)	nails
4	lose/put on	d)	hair
5	paint your	e)	make-up
6	put highlights	f)	beard
7	shave your	g)	your hairstyle
8	not wear	h)	head/legs

2 Label the pictures with phrases from Exercise 1.

1 *dye your hair*

2 ______

3 ______

4 ______

5 ______

6 ______

Grammar: Present Perfect

➤ Grammar Reference, page 107

☆ **3 Write the Present Perfect form of the verbs. Then write R (Regular) or I (Irregular).**

1 change *have changed R*
2 cut *have cut I*
3 dye ______
4 finish ______
5 grow ______
6 lose ______
7 paint ______
8 put ______
9 shave ______

☆ **4 Look at the pictures. Are the sentences true (T) or false (F)?**

1 He's shaved his head. [F]
2 They've put on weight. [ ]
3 She's changed her hairstyle. [ ]
4 He's put on make-up. [ ]
5 He's grown a beard. [ ]
6 They've dyed their hair. [ ]
7 They haven't cut their hair. [ ]

☆☆ **5 Complete the sentences about Picture B. Use the Present Perfect.**

1 They *have lost* (lose) weight.
2 They ______ (get) different clothes.
3 She ______ (paint) her nails.
4 He ______ (not paint) his nails.
5 They ______ (not grow) their hair.
6 ______ she ______ (put on) make-up?
7 Yes, she ______ .
8 ______ he ______ (put on) earrings?
9 No, he ______ .

☆☆☆ **6 Use the prompts to write short dialogues.**

1 A You look different. *Have you changed* (you / change) your hairstyle?
B No, I ______ . But ______ (I / dye) it.
2 A Your brothers look cool. ______ (they / lose) some weight?
B Yes, they ______ . And ______ (they / cut) their hair.
3 A Your dad looks different. What ______ (he / do) ?
B ______ (he / shave) his head for charity.
4 A Are you ready for the party?
B Well, ______ (I / change) my dress and ______ (I / put on) some make-up but ______ (I / not paint) my nails.

Your Turn

7 What have you done recently? Write five sentences.

1 I've changed *my hairstyle* .
2 I've visited ______ .
3 ______ .
4 ______ .
5 ______ .
6 ______ .

17 Skills

Vocabulary: Clothes

1 Complete the crossword.

Across

Down

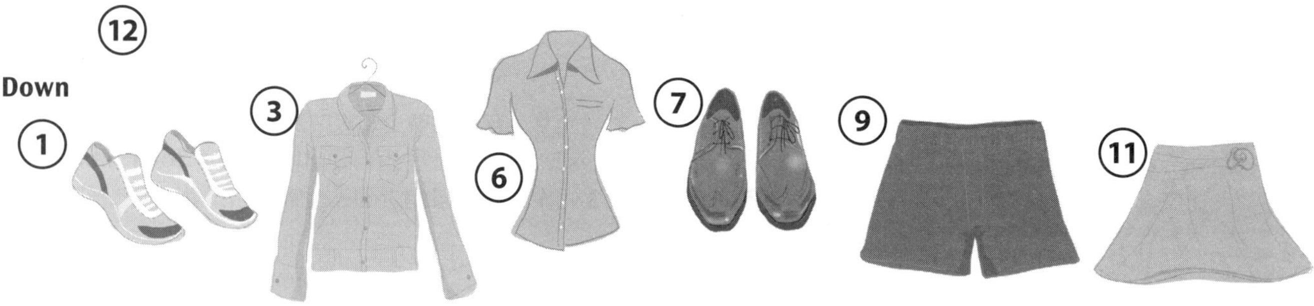

2 Complete the sentences with *on*, *up* or *out*.

Word Builder

1. Don't do *up* your shoelaces. It's cooler.
2. You can't put ______ make-up for school.
3. Have you tried ______ those jeans?
4. I want to find ______ where she buys her clothes.
5. Do ______ your trainers!

3 Rewrite the sentences in another way. Use the same verbs.

Sentence Builder

1. The teacher didn't give us a prize.
   The teacher didn't *give a prize to us* .
2. We sent an email to John.
   We sent ______ .
3. Did you tell the truth to me?
   Did you tell ______ ?
4. I'm writing my cousin a letter.
   I'm writing ______ .
5. My friend sent a postcard to me.
   My friend sent ______ .
6. I gave a present to my mum.
   I gave ______ .
7. Who gave you that bike?
   Who gave ______ ?
8. Sindy sent me a text message.
   Sindy sent ______ .

Reading

4 **Read the messages and choose a), b) or c).**

http://www.messenger.net/teentalk.asp

MESSENGER

Login

Lee, 14, London

At my school, there are groups of Goths, Rockers, Skaters and a lot more. Nobody can escape. We have to be something. This happens to everybody at secondary school, but even younger kids think they have to be part of a group.

In some ways this is okay. But in other ways I don't think it's good. Some people don't want to be sheep. They don't want to be part of a crowd. But it's very difficult – maybe impossible.

How do people choose their groups? I'm not really sure – but I think it's mostly because of music. Rock or Punk? Metal or R&B? These different styles of music control our lives.

What group am I in? What label have they given me? I don't know, but I'm sure I've got one. I don't want to be 'cool' or 'uncool' just because of my favourite music. I just want to be me.

Dave from Bristol

I'm 15 and everybody in my year at school has a label like Goth or Punk or something. I've got dyed black hair so I'm called a Goth, but I don't usually wear black so I'm not really one. I don't like giving people labels.

Clare G

Hi. I'm not in any group. I've got Goth clothes and Punk clothes and other kinds too and I like all kinds of music. Who cares?

1 Everybody at Lee's school is part of a group.
a) True **b)** False **c)** Doesn't Say

2 The groups begin at secondary school.
a) True **b)** False **c)** Doesn't Say

3 Lee thinks the groups are a bad thing for everybody.
a) True **b)** False **c)** Doesn't Say

4 He likes Rock music.
a) True **b)** False **c)** Doesn't Say

5 He thinks he's in a group.
a) True **b)** False **c)** Doesn't Say

6 Dave thinks he's a Goth.
a) True **b)** False **c)** Doesn't Say

7 Clare likes being in a group.
a) True **b)** False **c)** Doesn't Say

Writing

5 **Write your own messages about style. Complete the sentences.**

Sentence Builder

Hi! I think ____________________ .

Hi! I don't think ____________________ .

18 Communication

Vocabulary

1 **Match the two parts of the phrases.**

1	Did you buy	a)	okay.
2	I think it's	b)	think?
3	Oh,	c)	anything?
4	What about	d)	you?
5	What do you	e)	stop it!

2 **Complete the dialogues with the phrases in Exercise 1.**

1 A Do you like my new shirt?
B [1] *I think it's okay.*
A Okay! It's better than okay!

2 A I went into town today.
B [2] ________
A Yes, I got these jeans and this T-shirt.
[3] ________
B No, I didn't buy anything. I haven't got any money.

3 A Look, I've got a new dress.
[4] ________
B It really suits you. And you've painted your nails and put on some make-up. Have you got a date tonight?
B Yes, I have.
A Oh, who with?
B [5] ________

3 **Rewrite the sentences in another way. Use the words in the box.**

Sentence Builder

baggy ~~cheap~~ dark long small

1 This top is too expensive.
It *isn't cheap enough* .
2 These jeans are too tight.
They ________ .
3 Is this skirt too short?
Is it ________ ?
4 Is this shirt light enough?
Is it ________ ?
5 These shoes aren't big enough.
They're ________ .

Key Expressions: Shopping

4 **Complete the dialogues. Write one word in each gap.**

Shop assistant	Can I [1] *help* you?
Customer	Thanks. I like this T-shirt. What [2] ________ is it?
Shop assistant	That one's small.
Customer	How [3] ________ is it?
Shop assistant	£15.
Customer	Do you think the colour is okay for me?
Shop assistant	Oh yes, it really [4] ________ you.
Customer	Can I [5] ________ it on, please?
Shop assistant	Yes of course. The [6] ________ room is over there.
Customer	Thank you.

Shop assistant	Can I help you?
Customer	Yes, I'm [7] ________ for a pair of shoes?
Shop assistant	What [8] ________ are you?
Customer	I am a 38.
Shop assistant	Do you think this colour is okay for you?
Customer	Oh yes, I like it. Can I [9] ________ them on, please?
Shop assistant	Yes, of course. Take a seat.
Customer	[10] ________ you.

Listening

26 **5 Listen and choose the correct answers.**

1 How much are the trainers?

a) ☐

b) ☑

c) ☐

2 What colour top does she try?

red	blue	green
a) ☐	b) ☐	c) ☐

3 What does he buy?

a) ☐

b) ☐

c) ☐

4 What does the shop sell?

jazz	jazz and folk	jazz, folk and classical
a) ☐	b) ☐	c) ☐

5 Which game is the best?

a) ☐

b) ☐

c) ☐

Writing Challenge 3

1 **Read the blog. Choose the correct words.**

• **Saturday 11th August**

Well here we are in Scotland. [1]*During/When* the journey THREE people were sick on the bus, so we were all very happy [2]*then/when* we arrived! The hostel is great – it's quite small and it's in the middle of nowhere! There are six of us in each room. No time to write more – dinner time! I'm REALLY hungry.

• **Monday 13th August**

Yesterday started well, but then something horrible happened. In the morning we got ready to go walking. [3]*Before/During* we left the hostel, the teachers checked our equipment. Each group had a map and an emergency bag with a mobile phone and some food.

Our problems started [4]*during/when* we got lost. Ben Williams decided to go and look for the others. This was a BIG mistake! We waited and waited but he didn't come back, so we decided to use the emergency mobile. Then we [5]*later/suddenly* remembered – Ben was carrying it!

Honestly, it was terrible. We were really scared. We tried to find the hostel but it was getting dark and we were going round in circles. [6]*After/Later* about an hour one of the teachers found us. [7]*After/Later*, we found out that Ben had a broken leg and was in hospital.

• **Wednesday 15th August**

We went to see Ben in hospital today. He's okay but he's really bored. He'll be there for a week. His parents are travelling to Scotland – they'll take him home [8]*when/later* he's a bit better.

2 **Read the blog again and answer the questions.**

1 Where were they? *in a hostel in Scotland*
2 Why were they there? ______________
3 What happened? ______________
4 How did they feel? ______________
5 What happened in the end? ______________

3 **Write a blog about a terrible week. It can be true, or you can imagine it.**

Understanding Grammar: *must* and *mustn't*

➤ Grammar Reference, page 108

☆ **1 Complete the sentences. Choose a), b) or c).**

1 It's 3 o'clock in the morning. You *b* to bed.
 a) mustn't to go
 b) must go
 c) must

2 He's running in the sun. He ___ a lot of water.
 a) mustn't drink
 b) must drink
 c) must drinks

3 She's got pierced ears. She ___ them clean.
 a) must keeping
 b) must keeps
 c) must keep

4 Doctor, our baby is very ill. You ___ us!
 a) must help
 b) mustn't help
 c) help

5 The cat's got plump. It ___ more weight.
 a) puts on
 b) mustn't put on
 c) must put on

6 Why ___ a doctor?
 a) must I see
 b) I must see
 c) must see

☆ **2 Put the words in the correct order to make sentences.**

1 mustn't / in / we / mobiles / use / lessons
 We mustn't use mobiles in lessons.

2 her / do / must / homework / she
 ______

3 I / for / late / arrive / exam / mustn't / the
 ______

4 earrings / wear / at / he / mustn't / school
 ______

5 a / must / from / letter / you / bring / parents / your
 ______

6 help / teachers / must / students / their
 ______

☆☆☆ **3 Look at the pictures. Write sentences with *must* or *mustn't*.**

1 you / go in the sun
2 you / stay in the house
 You mustn't go in the sun.
 You must stay in the house.

3 she / use the make-up again
4 she / see her doctor
 ______
 ______

5 they / take some water
6 they / go without a map
 ______
 ______

Language Check 6

Vocabulary

1 Find the odd one out.

	old	*middle-aged*	*young*	*(short)*
1	thin	teenager	short	tall
2	plump	blond	dark	fair
3	long	round	grey	square
4	handsome	good-looking	pretty	slim
5	fat	curly	straight	long
6	beard	skin	moustache	hair
7	cut	dyed	shaved	curly

☐ / 7

2 Complete the sentences with words for clothes.

It's cold! Put on your coat.

1 I can't walk fast because my s _ _ _ _ are too tight.
2 Jenny bought a new bl _ _ _ _ to wear with her new sk _ _ _ .
3 Boys don't wear d _ _ _ _ es, but girls can wear j _ _ ns!

☐ / 5

3 Choose the correct words.

You must do on/out/(up) your shoes. You don't want to fall over.

1 Why did you try *on/out/up* twelve pairs of shorts?
2 We've found *on/out/up* who he's got a date with.
3 My mum puts *on/out/up* make-up every morning.

☐ / 3

Grammar

4 Write the sentences in the Present Perfect.

you / see / John today?
Have you seen John today?

1 Nobody / send / me a text message this week!
____
2 Look – Sarah / dye / her hair!
____
3 Sorry. I / not / finish / my homework.
____
4 you / buy / that new CD?
____
5 Oh no! I / lose / my mobile again.
____

☐ / 5

5 Complete the sentences with *must* or *mustn't*.

You must keep pierced ears clean.

1 You ________ do an allergy test before you dye your hair.
2 You ________ stay in the sun for a long time. It's bad for your skin.
3 You ________ ride your skateboard without a helmet.
4 You ________ wear that skirt at school again. It's too short and it's too tight.
5 You ________ put on a coat. It's very cold outside.

☐ / 5

Key Expressions

6 Number the lines of the dialogue in the correct order.

A	**Assistant**	What size are you?	☐
B	**Customer**	Thanks.	☐
C	**Assistant**	Can I help you?	*1*
D	**Assistant**	Okay. What about this one? It's bigger.	☐
E	**Customer**	Yes, I'm looking for a T-shirt.	☐
F	**Customer**	Medium. Do you have a yellow one?	☐
G	**Customer**	No, it's not big enough.	☐
H	**Assistant**	Sure, the changing room is over there.	☐
I	**Customer**	Oh, all right. Can I try it on?	☐
J	**Assistant**	You're welcome.	☐
K	**Assistant**	Yellow? What about this one?	☐

☐ / 10

What's your score?

Module 6

☐ Vocabulary
☐ Grammar
☐ Key Expressions
☐ / 35

This is easy.
I need more practice.
This is difficult.

Module 7 Technology

Get Ready

Vocabulary: Technology (1)

27 **1** **Listen to the results of a raffle. Match the tickets (1–6) and the prizes (a–f).**

(a) 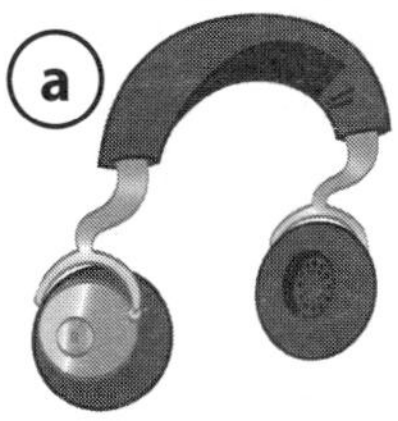

(b) 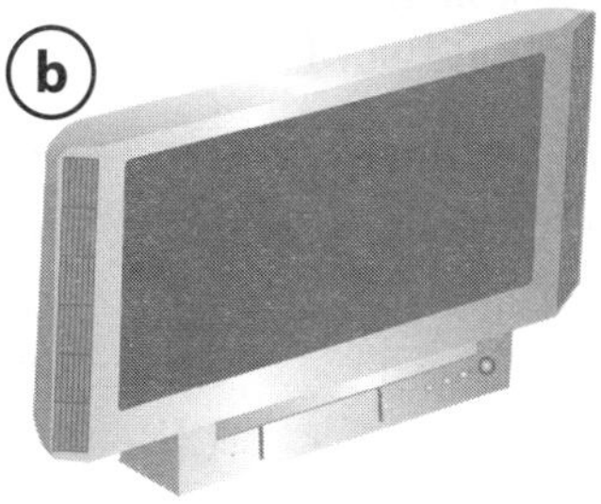

(c) 

(d) 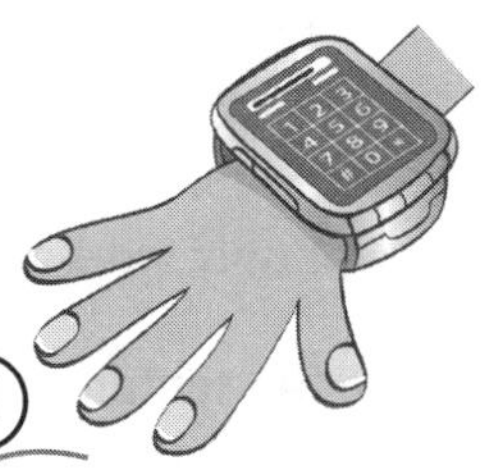

(e) 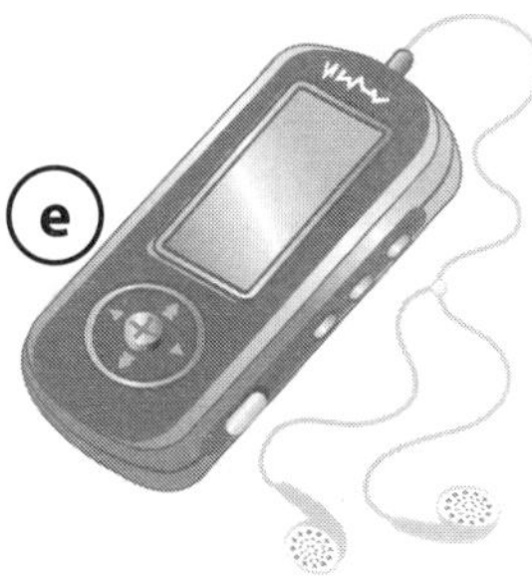

(f) 

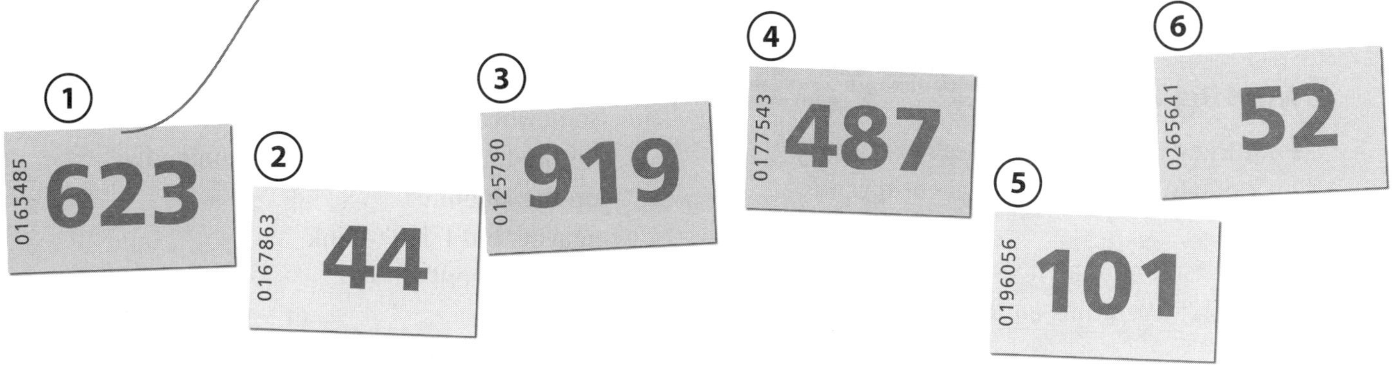

2 **What do they need? Choose things in the box.**

~~Blu-ray player~~ flat screen TV GPS pen drive wireless headset mobile with video camera

1 I want to watch a film at home.
Blu-ray player

2 My project is on the computer at school. I want to save it somewhere different, to keep it safe.

____

3 I want to record my family on holiday.

____

4 We want a really good TV picture.

____

5 I don't want to get lost!

____

6 I want to listen to my music on the train.

____

28 **3** **Linda and Tony are looking at a catalogue of gadgets. What things are they talking about?**

a) laptop
b) MP3 player
c) handheld computer
d) watch phone

1 [*c*]
2 [ ]
3 [ ]
4 [ ]

19 Vocabulary and Grammar

Vocabulary: Technology (2)

1 **Match the words (1–5) and (a–h) to make new words.**

1	artificial	a)	travel
2	colour	b)	paper
3	lap	c)	intelligence
4	news	d)	photograph
5	time	e)	top

2 **Write the new words in the correct columns.**

one word	two words
	artificial intelligence

3 **Read the sentences and complete the adjectives.**

Word Builder

1 Mickey is very sad; he's really un*happy* .
2 Nobody knows anything about this; it's un________ .
3 This isn't normal; it's very un________ .
4 I don't like sitting on this chair; it's very un________ .
5 This sandwich tastes horrible; it's very un________ .

Grammar: *will* for predictions

➤ Grammar Reference, page 109

THE DAILY NEWS
OCTOBER 9, 1950

WHAT WILL THE WORLD BE LIKE IN THE YEAR 2000?

☆ **4** **Read these predictions from 1950. Were they correct? Write true (T) or false (F).**

1 There will be one computer in every town. *F*
2 Millions of people will have colour TVs. *T*
3 Nobody will be poor or hungry. ☐
4 People will live in space stations. ☐
5 Robots will do all our housework. ☐
6 People will carry telephones in their pockets. ☐
7 There will be one world language. ☐
8 There won't be any wars in the world. ☐
9 The world will be warmer. ☐
10 People will only work three days a week. ☐

☆☆ **5** **Complete the sentences. Use the correct form of *will* and the verb in brackets.**

1 'Where *will you be* (you / be) in five years' time?'
'I think __________ (I / be) at university somewhere.'
2 'In the future, __________ (people / live) on the Moon?'
'Maybe, but I don't think __________ (I / volunteer)!'
3 'What time __________ (it / get) dark tonight?'
'I'm not sure, but I'm sure __________ (it / be) dark at about seven.'
4 'When __________ (you / be) 18?'
'In four years' time.'
5 'What __________ (cars / be) like in the future?'
'There __________ (not / be) any cars, because we __________ (not / have) any petrol.'
6 '__________ (we / have) robots to do the housework in twenty years time?'
'Yes, of course. __________ (we / have) robots to do everything!'
7 'How long __________ (you / be) away?'
'For one month. __________ (I / see) you in September.'
8 '__________ (you / help) me set up my new laptop?'
'Okay. __________ (I / come) to your house on Saturday. Alright?'

6 **What do they think? Write their predictions.**

1 safer streets – no street crime

2 cleaner planet – electric cars – healthier life

3 no schools – virtual classrooms – people more intelligent

4 different weather – colder winters, hotter summers – more sunshine in Britain

5 better buses and trains – free transport for everybody – no cars

Your Turn

7 **Imagine cars, computers and towns in the year 2050. Make predictions.**

cars *I think* ______________________

____

____

computers ______________________

____

____

towns ______________________

____

____

8 **Answer the question. Use the words in the box or your own ideas.**

animals doctors the Earth houses hunger the Moon planets pollution robots schools space trees wars the weather

What do **you** think life will be like in 2050?

I think ______________________

____

____

____

____

20 Skills

Vocabulary

1 Write the adjectives.

1 c *o n f u s e d*
2 sc _ r _ d
3 r _ _ gh
4 pl _ _ s _ d
5 s _ r _ _ _ s
6 _ nh _ _ py
7 b _ s _
8 _ nc _ _ nt

2 Use the words in Exercise 1 to write about the pictures.

1 They were *confused* in their maths lesson.

2 The sea was ________ .

3 She is very ________ .

4 He was ________ when he opened his present.

5 It was ________ news.

6 She was ________ when she heard a strange noise.

3 Choose the correct words.

1 The teacher *landed/picked up/turned* her books and left the classroom.
2 When the aeroplane *picked up/landed/took off* all the passengers got off.
3 My grandmother can't hear very well so she *ignores/struggles/turns* the dial on her TV to LOUD.
4 Our dog *struggles/lands/takes off* when we wash him.
5 The star's fans were waiting in the rain but she *landed/turned/ignored* them and got into her car.

4 Complete the Sentence Builder with the words in the box.

Sentence Builder

~~big~~ fast high long many much old

1 How *big* is your laptop's screen?
It's 39.5 cms.
2 How ________ is your mobile?
I bought it two years ago.
3 How ________ songs can you put on an MP3 player?
I don't know. Thousands!
4 How ________ is a memory stick?
A cheap one is about £10.
5 How ________ has your family had a home cinema system?
About six months.
6 How ________ is your wi-fi?
It's very slow sometimes.
7 How ________ is the mobile tower near your house?
It's twenty metres from top to bottom.

Reading

5 **Complete the text. Choose a), b) or c).**

1	a) a	(b) the	c) some
2	a) to	b) up	c) through
3	a) in	b) at	c) on
4	a) no	b) some	c) any
5	a) so	b) but	c) because
6	a) Who	b) Where	c) Why
7	a) do	b) did	c) are doing

A Very Unusual Doctor

Doctor Who is one of [1] *b* most famous TV shows in Britain. It's a science fiction story about an alien 'time traveller' (the Doctor) and his young assistant. They travel [2] ___ space and time in a very unusual 'spaceship' – it's a blue phone box! To find out more, we have to go back many years (like the Doctor!).

The first *Doctor Who* show appeared on British screens [3] ___ 1963. In those days, there were two kinds of phone box – red ones and special blue ones. The blue ones were for emergencies. People used them to call the police, and policemen used them, too. The writers of *Doctor Who* wanted the Doctor's spaceship to be an everyday object – and they picked a blue phone box (it's called 'the Tardis' in the show). These days, there aren't [4] ___ blue phone boxes on British streets, [5] ___ Doctor Who still travels in one!

The Tardis is always the same, but the actors often change. In the story, Doctor Who sometimes disappears, and then reappears with a different body! His assistants sometimes change, too – but his worst enemies don't. [6] ___ are they? They are metal robots on wheels, and they are called 'the Daleks'. They look and sound strange (and funny) – but they always try to kill the Doctor, so they are terrifying! In the sixties, children watched the Daleks from behind the sofa. These days, they [7] ___ the same!

6 **Read the text again. Find words with these meanings:**

Paragraph 1

1 a person on a journey
traveller

Paragraph 2

2 ordinary
______

3 chose
______

Paragraph 3

4 comes back
______

5 very scary
______

21 Communication

Vocabulary

1 Complete the crossword.

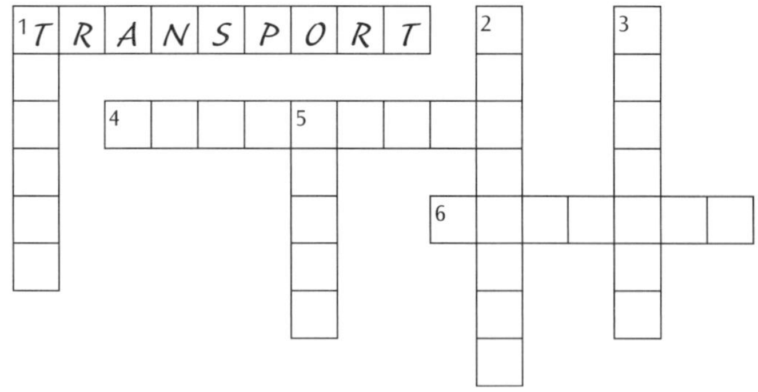

Across
1 This means buses, trains, cars, planes, bikes, etc.
4 Stand on these when you wait for trains.
6 Go to this office for information about a new place.

Down
1 Buy this before you travel.
2 This means a special cheap price.
3 Go here when you want to travel by train.
5 A river bus.

Key Expressions: Asking for tourist information

2 Complete the dialogue. Choose correct replies for B. There are two extra replies.

A Can I help you?
B 1 ___b___
A Certainly. Do you want to go by train or bus?
B 2 ______
A Bus. It's £15, and the train is £40. But the bus takes longer. Are you in a hurry?
B 3 ______
A Four o'clock. They go every hour. You've got time for a coffee first.
B 4 ______
A Yes, 15 per cent, with a student card.
B 5 ______
A It's over there.
B 6 ______
A That's okay. Have a good journey.

a) I don't know. Which is cheaper?
b) Yes, please. I'd like some information about transport to London.
c) How long does it take?
d) Thanks very much. Bye.
e) Great, I've got one! So, where's the ticket office?
f) No, I'm not. What time's the next bus?
g) Good idea! And can I get a student discount?
h) Yes, I do.

Listening

29 **3 Listen to the station announcements. Answer the questions.**

(1)
What time is the next train to Oxford, please?
9.42
Thanks. Which platform do I need?
____

(2)
I want to go to Birmingham. When's the next train?
____
Thanks. Where will it go from?
Platform __________

(3)
I'm meeting a friend from Manchester. Where will the train arrive, please?
Platform __________

(4)
Excuse me. I'm waiting for somebody from London. What time is the next train?
____
Thanks. Which platform will that be?
____

30 **4 Listen to the announcement. Complete the notes.**

London express			
food and drinks from carriage number	1 *2*		
get food and drink from	2 _____	to	3 _____
no mobiles in carriage number	4 _____		
arrival time	5 _____		

31 **5 Listen to tourist information about Cambridge. Complete the notes.**

Bus tickets	
single	£ *2.00*
'all day'	1 £ _____
tourist	2 £ _____
student discounts? (yes/no)	3 _____

Cycling	
rent a bike	4 £ _____
for one	5 _____

Boat trips (punting)		
take a boat out	6 £ _____	an hour
for each	7 £ _____	
take a trip	8 £ _____	
for each	9 £ _____	

Reading Corner 4

1 Read and choose a), b) or c).

The article is about …

a) how to win some money.
b) a competition.
c) a clever idea.

Q What do a lot of successful inventors share?
A They all started their businesses when they were teenagers.

The Young Designers Competition encourages students aged from 13 to 16 to design new, exciting things.

The competition started in 2008 and more than 4,000 teenagers enter it every year. Rose Steadman organises the competition. 'I have a fantastic job. Every year, I meet a lot of very clever teenagers with great ideas. For example, last year, a girl in Norfolk made a solar powered cold bag for food. The year before, a boy from Devon designed a recycled wood toy box for young children.'

The first winner was Jason Owen. In 2009, when he was fourteen, Jason designed and made a picnic bag – for a dog! Jason explained where his idea came from. 'My dad can't see so he has a guide dog. I made the first bag with denim from some old jeans but now they are nylon – it's easier to clean. I designed them for working dogs but now people buy them for their family pets. It was really exciting when I won. It gave me a lot of confidence and the prize money was very useful! I used it to advertise the pet picnic bag.'

Lola Bennett was the winner in 2010. She wanted to practise speaking Spanish but she was worried about just looking on the Internet and using social networking sites. Her answer to the problem? She designed a language exchange website for students all over the world. Lola says, 'I started the website when I was fourteen and now there are 750,000 members. I designed it for students aged thirteen to sixteen and it's a safe social networking site.'

Brother and sister Leanne and Jacob Nelson also invented something to solve a problem. Their great-grandmother couldn't use a computer mouse because her hands were too old. 'The mouse was very uncomfortable for her. It was too small. We designed a cover so she could use it easily. We made it with some foam from an old bed. A computer company bought the idea from us a year ago. Now we're thinking about what we can do next to help her and other old people use technology.'

2 Are the sentences about the text true (T) or false (F)?

1 There is a Young Designers Competition two times a year. F
2 Rose Steadman likes her job. ☐
3 Mr Owen, Jason's dad, has a dog to help him. ☐
4 Jason designed his dog picnic bag because he wanted to win a lot of money. ☐
5 Lola designed her website because she was studying Spanish. ☐
6 Lola's social network site isn't for adults. ☐
7 Leanne and Jacob's great-grandmother didn't know how to use a computer. ☐
8 Leanne and Jacob have sold their idea. ☐
9 Leanne and Jacob want to invent more things to help people. ☐

3 Complete the table with words from the text.

verb	noun (person)
to design	a designer
to invent	an ________
to win	a ________

4 Complete the sentences with the correct form of the words in brackets.

1 Tim Berners-Lee *invented* the World Wide Web in 1989. (invent)
2 The ________ of the Millennium Technology Prize gets €800,000. (win)
3 Paul McCartney's daughter Stella ________ clothes. (design)
4 Marie Curie ________ two Nobel prizes for science: one in 1903 and another in 1911. (win)
5 The ________ of the London Eye were David Marks and Julia Barfield. (design)
6 Mark Zuckerman is the ________ of the world's biggest social network site. (invent)

5 Complete the materials.

1 a f *o* *a* m bed

2 a n _ l _ n rucksack

3 a recycled w _ _ d chair

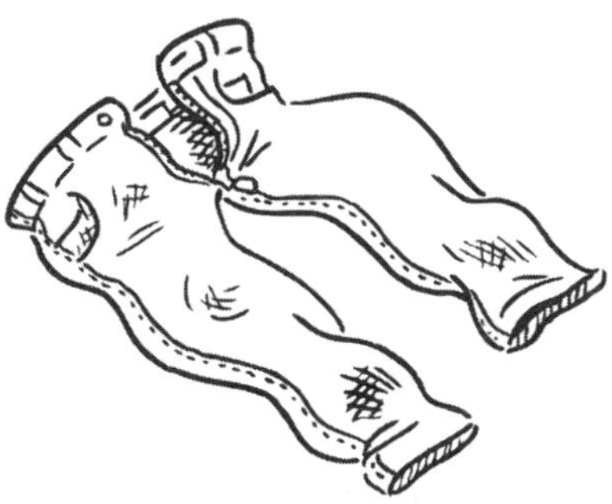

4 some d _ n _ m jeans

5 a p _ _ s _ _ c bottle

6 a m _ t _ l watch

6 Read the problems and the example answer. Write your ideas.

problems	answers
1 I've got a lot of exams!	*design a website with a study timetable*
2 I can't remember English words!	
3 I lose my mobile every day!	
4 I ...	
5 I ...	

* HELP! English mobile Phone! exams

Language Check 7

Vocabulary

1 Complete the words (a–f), then match them with words (1–6).

1	digital	*f*	a	h _ _ _ _ _ t
2	wireless		b	s _ _ _ _ n TV
3	MP3		c	p _ _ _ _ r
4	flat		d	c _ _ _ _ _ _ _ r
5	interactive		e	t _ _ _ h t _ _ _ e
6	handheld		f	c *a m e r a*

☐ / 10

2 Complete the adjectives.

I hate these shoes. They're uncomfortable.

1 A fish and chocolate ice cream? That sounds un________ .
2 She never smiles. She's always un________ .
3 He isn't un________ . His picture is in all the newspapers.
4 All the students got 100 per cent in the test. That's un________ .
5 I don't like sleeping in this bed. It's un________ .

☐ / 5

Grammar

3 Put the verbs in brackets in the correct form.

I can't be late. My parents will get (get) angry.

1 Please wait for me. I ________ (not / be) long.
2 Do you think we ________ (win) the match tomorrow?
3 What time ________ (you / finish) your homework tonight?'
4 Take a coat. It ________ (be) cold tonight.
5 Eat something now, then you ________ (not / be) hungry this evening.

☐ / 5

4 Put the words in the correct order to make sentences.

1 I'll / in / four / time / years' / be / at / university

____

2 won't / in / future / any / there / be / money / the

____

3 your / will / this / mum / love / present / birthday

____

4 football match / me / you / to / take / the / on / Saturday / will / ?

____

5 finish / won't / to / the exam / have / we / time

____

(2 points for each question) ☐ / 10

Key Expressions

5 Complete the dialogue in a tourist information office. Write one word in each gap.

A I'd *like* some information, please. [1]________ can we catch the bus to Buckingham Palace?
B The bus goes [2]________ the bus stop over there. Get [3]________ at Trafalgar Square and walk down The Mall.
A I've got one more question. How do we [4]________ to Oxford Street from there?
B You can catch the number 16 bus to Hyde Park Corner.
A Are there any [5]________ for young people?
B Yes, there are. Students can get cheaper tickets.

☐ / 5

What's your score?

Module 7

☐ Vocabulary
☐ Grammar
☐ Key Expressions
☐ / 35

This is easy.
I need more practice.
This is difficult.

Module 8 Holidays

Get Ready

Vocabulary: Holiday activities

1 **Look at the pictures and complete the text.**

Last summer, I [1] *went*  *camping* with some friends. On the first day, we [2] ________ to the  [3] ________. I [4] ________  ________ and my friend Tessa [5] ________  ________. Sam [6] ________  ________. On the second day we [7] ________  ________ in the morning, and we [8] ________  ________ in the afternoon. The next day it rained, so we [9] ________ to a  [10] ________! Our tent was very wet so after that we [11] ________ at a  [12] ________.

2 **Read the postcards and answer the questions. Write Jo, Pete or Sara.**

a

It's great here. Our tent is really big and the other people are friendly. We're near the sea. Yesterday I caught a fish and we cooked it for dinner!
See you soon, Jo x

Affix stamp here

Jeremy Clark
19 Andover St.
Eltham
London

b

This place is brilliant. I've got an enormous bed and there's a TV in my room! This morning we rented some bikes and had a fantastic time, then came back for a VERY nice lunch!
Love, Pete

c

We're all having a good time here. Yesterday I went skiing but I was terrible! This morning we went to Edinburgh – it's a great city. I've got HUNDREDS of photos!
Bye for now
Sara

Who …

went fishing?	1 *Jo*
went sightseeing?	2 ________
went cycling?	3 ________
went skiing?	4 ________
is staying at a campsite?	5 ________
is staying at a hotel?	6 ________

Listening

32 **3** **Listen to the advertisements (1–3) and match them with the postcards (a–c) in Exercise 2.**

1 The Activity Holiday Company [*c*]
2 Medvac Holidays [ ]
3 Raymond's [ ]

33 **4** **Listen again. Are the sentences true (T) or false (F)?**

The Activity Holiday Company

1 You have a holiday in Scotland. [*T*]
2 You stay in a hotel. [ ]

Medvac Holidays

3 You take your tent with you. [ ]
4 This holiday is fine for children. [ ]

Raymond's

5 You can play sport at Raymond's. [ ]
6 Raymond's is next to an amusement park. [ ]

22 Vocabulary and Grammar

Vocabulary

1 **Complete the words.**

1 p *o* *s* tc *a* *r* d

2 b __ __ k c __ __ d

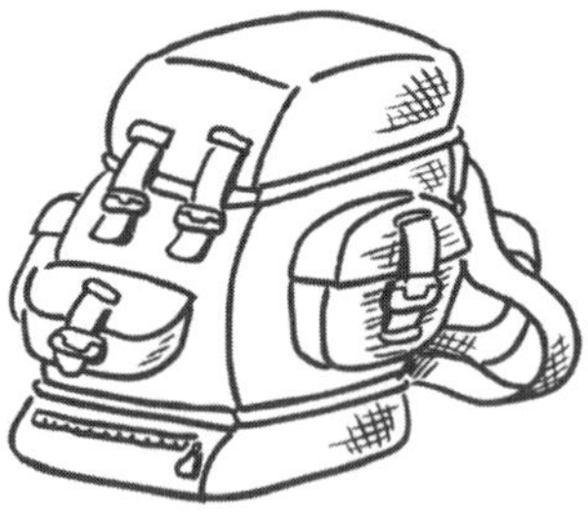

3 r __ __ __ __ __ __ __ k

4 l __ __ t

5 c __ __ h

6 p __ __ __ __ __ __ __ t

2 **Complete the phrases with the words in the box.**

book ~~get~~ give go (x 2) have pack plan write

1 *get* a haircut
2 ________ a list
3 ________ a bag
4 ________ someone a lift
5 ________ a hostel
6 ________ to the dentist
7 ________ a driving lesson
8 ________ a holiday
9 ________ on holiday

Grammar: Arrangements and intentions

▶ Grammar Reference, page 110

☆ **3** **Read the sentences. Write A (arrangement) or I (intention).**

1 I'm going to pack a lot of warm clothes. *I*
2 We're meeting at the bus station. ___
3 He's going to buy a Spanish/English dictionary. ___
4 She's flying on Saturday evening. ___
5 They aren't going to stay in a hotel. ___
6 I'm not working this summer. ___

☆☆ **4** **Read Esther's list about her holiday plans. Complete the dialogue.**

Camping holiday
~~buy a tent~~ x share Ruby's
borrow a sleeping bag
pack a water bottle
buy some comfortable shoes
~~pack some food~~
take a map

Millie Are you ready for our holiday?

Esther Well, I've written a list. I [1] *'m not going to buy a tent*. I [2] ________ Ruby's.

Millie I hope she doesn't mind! What about a sleeping bag?

Esther I [3] ________ a sleeping bag from my brother. I don't want to buy one.

Millie [4] ________ you ________ any food or drinks?

Esther No, I [5] ________ any food. It's too heavy. But I [6] ________ a water bottle. I can fill it at the campsite.

Millie Good idea. I need some walking shoes. Have you got any?

Esther No, I haven't. Ruby and I [7] ________ comfortable shoes at the weekend.

Millie Can I come with you? I want to get a map as well.

Esther You don't need to buy one. I [8] ________ a map.

Millie You with a map! We're going to need GPS too!

5 Read the arrangements for a school trip to London. Complete what the teacher tells the class.

7.30: coach leaves school
9.15: stop for 15 minutes at motorway cafe
10.30: arrive at the Science Museum
10.45: visit Teen Inventors Exhibition
~~12.15: have lunch at the Science Museum~~
12.30: have picnic lunch in Hyde Park
~~13.30: go on walking tour~~
13.30: go on open-top bus tour of the main sights, including Oxford Street, Trafalgar Square, St Paul's Cathedral and Piccadilly Circus finishing at Big Ben
15.00: start tour of the Houses of Parliament
16.15: coach meets us in Parliament Square

'Listen carefully, I'm going to tell you about the arrangements for Tuesday's visit to London. The coach [1] *is leaving* school at 7.30. Don't be late! We're not waiting for anyone! The journey takes three hours so the coach [2] ________ at 9.15 so we can get drinks and go to the toilet.

We [3] ________ at the Science Museum at 10.30 and we [4] ________ the Teen Inventors Exhibition at 10.45.

We've changed the plan for lunch: we [5] ________ it at the Science Museum. Instead, we [6] ________ a picnic lunch in Hyde Park so remember to bring some sandwiches.

OK, after lunch, at half past one, we [7] ________ on a walking tour, we [8] ________ an open-top bus tour of the main sights. The bus tour [9] ________ at Big Ben, next to the Houses of Parliament. We [10] ________ our visit to the Houses of Parliament at three o'clock. It lasts one hour.

The coach [11] ________ us in Parliament Square at a quarter past four.

Any questions?'

6 Sally is a tour leader. Look at her year planner and complete the sentences. Use *be going to* or the Present Continuous.

March
5th take a group of international students camping
17th (with Dan) teach a surfing course
Notes
train for the London Marathon!
buy wetsuit for surfing course
get new running shoes

April
12th (with Cleo) do an activity weekend for young criminals
~~14th teach a climbing course~~
lead a walking tour in the Lake District.
20th run the London Marathon
22nd go on holiday!
Notes
train for the London Marathon!
buy a new camera for my holiday

1 On 5th March she*'s taking a group of students camping.*
2 On 17th March Sally and Dan ________ .
3 In March and April, she ________ but she doesn't know when.
4 Some time in March she ________ and ________ .
5 On 12th April, Sally and Cleo ________ .
6 Her plans for the 14th April have changed. She ________ a climbing course. She ________ in the Lake District.
7 On 20th April, she ________ .
8 Two days after the Marathon, she ________ .
9 Before that, she ________ a new camera.

Reading

1 Read the text and choose a), b) or c).

Extreme Winter Sports – ICE DIVING

Ice diving is a sport for expert divers – and crazy ones, too!

Before you go ice diving, you put on special warm clothes and then you put on a special diving suit called a 'drysuit'. This is not the same as a normal diving suit. It has air in it. The air keeps the diver warm, and also keeps him (or her) high in the water. Ice divers carry oxygen on their backs, like normal divers.

A typical ice dive takes fifteen minutes. The diver climbs into a hole in the ice and then swims under it. The other divers watch and wait. They are ready to help in an emergency. They can't see the diver, but they can often see his air bubbles under the ice.

So, what's it like, under the ice? Ice divers say it's like another world – a bright world of strange creatures, plants and rocks and amazing shapes and colours. It's also great fun. Divers can turn over and put their feet on the ice. When their friends pull the rope, they move along, with their feet higher than their heads!

An ice diver goes down into the icy water

1 Ice diving is NOT a sport for most people.
   (a) Right b) Wrong c) Doesn't say
2 Ice divers wear clothes under their drysuits.
   a) Right b) Wrong c) Doesn't say
3 Their oxygen is inside their drysuits.
   a) Right b) Wrong c) Doesn't say
4 They usually dive for about a quarter of an hour.
   a) Right b) Wrong c) Doesn't say
5 Emergencies don't happen very often.
   a) Right b) Wrong c) Doesn't say
6 It's dark under the ice.
   a) Right b) Wrong c) Doesn't say
7 Divers go ice diving because it's fun.
   a) Right b) Wrong c) Doesn't say

Vocabulary: Opinion Adjectives

2 **Read the text again. Complete the adjectives.**

1 Ice divers are a *d v e n t u r o u s*, b r _ _ e and c _ _ z _ !
2 Under the ice it is a _ _ z _ _ g, b _ _ u _ _ _ _ l and w _ _ _ _ r _ _ l.
3 Ice diving is d _ _ _ _ r _ _ s, and s _ _ r _ – but it's e _ c _ _ _ _ g and e _ j _ _ _ _ _ e, too!
4 The hotel is l _ v _ _ y and the holiday is g r _ _ _ .

3 Choose the correct words.

Word Builder

1. Be careful! There's *ice/icy* on the road. It's *danger/dangerous.*
2. We had a great *adventure/adventurous.* It was very *enjoy/enjoyable.*
3. Look after your *health/healthy.* Eat *health/healthy* food like fruit and vegetables.
4. Norway is a *north/northern* country. The *north/northern* of Norway is in the Arctic Circle.
5. Sam loves being *act/active.* He's very *adventure/adventurous.*

4 Complete the questions (1–6) with *much* or *many*. Then match them with the correct answers (a–f).

Sentence Builder

1. How *much* were the skiing lessons? [*f*]
2. How ________ snow was there? [ ]
3. How ________ time did you spend in the sauna? [ ]
4. How ________ times did you fall in the snow? [ ]
5. How ________ people slept in the igloo? [ ]
6. How ________ photos did you take? [ ]

a. There were three of us.
b. Millions! I'm terrible at skiing.
c. A lot! Do you want to see them?
d. There was a lot!
e. About half an hour.
f. They were £50.

5 Read the advertisement. Complete the notes.

country: 1 *Iceland*

dates: 2 ________

city: 3 ________

accommodation: 4 ________

activities: 5 ________

cost: 6 ________

6 Complete the sentence. Use the information in Exercise 5 or your own ideas.

I'd like/I wouldn't like to go to Iceland because

____

____

____

____

24 Communication

Vocabulary

1 Complete the dialogues. Use the words in the box.

fun impossible remember ~~right~~ stop it teasing

A Come on. You look okay.
B Yes, you're 1 _right_ . I look fantastic!
A You're 2 ________ !

A I'm going to France on Eurostar with my aunt and uncle.
B That'll be 3 ________ . Do you know you wear a wetsuit in the train tunnel?
A What!
B I'm only 4 ________ !

A 5 ________ to clean your teeth and brush your hair every day.
B Have you got your address book? You must send a postcard to Granddad.
C 6 ________ ! I'll be okay!

Key Expressions: Advice

2 Complete the advice to Jack.

1 _You should_ check the time of the train.
2 ________ get ready earlier.
3 ________ always be late.
4 ________ run across the road.

Your Turn

3 Give a visitor some advice about your town.

1 You should see ________ because ________ .
2 You shouldn't see ________ because ________ .

4 Complete the dialogue. Choose correct replies for Dan.

Tom Hi! Thanks for lending me your watch for my exam yesterday.
Dan 1 _c_
Tom It was fine, but there's just one problem.
Dan 2 ______
Tom I dropped your watch. I'm really sorry.
Dan 3 ______
Tom No, I don't think so. But it's got a mark on it.
Dan 4 ______
Tom Are you sure? I feel terrible.
Dan 5 ______
Tom Was it? Oh, good!
Dan 6 ______
Tom Well, thanks again!

a) Oh yes? What's that?
b) Yes, it was. So don't worry.
c) That's okay. How did it go?
d) Oh, is it broken?
e) Yes, I am. Don't worry. It was quite old.
f) Has it? Well, it doesn't matter.

5 What do you say? Write your own ideas.

1 You borrowed a friend's dictionary and now you can't find it.

You *I'm sorry. I'll look for it again tonight* . **Your friend** ____________ .

2 You put your friend's notebook in your bag by mistake. He can't do his homework without it.

You ____________ . **Your friend** ____________ .

3 Your friend's family invited you to dinner, but you forgot to go.

You ____________ . **Your friend** ____________ .

4 Your friend has helped you paint your bedroom.

You ____________ . **Your friend** ____________ .

Listening

34 **6 A visitor to London is asking for information about the Tower Bridge Exhibition. Listen and complete the information.**

open [1] *7* days a week
opening times 10 a.m. – [2] ________

Tickets
adults [3] ________
students [4] ________
children [5] ________
(under) [6] ________

website address www. [7] ________ .org.uk

35 **7 Listen and complete the information about the Tower Bridge Exhibition.**

In 1876 there was a competition to [1] *design a new bridge* . There were more than [2] ________ designs. It took [3] ________ to build the bridge. When a big ship needs to go under it, the traffic [4] ________ and the bridge [5] ________ . In 1952, a London bus [6] ________ . Visitors can [7] ________ and enjoy the views.

36 **8 Listen again and complete the postcard. Say what you did and what you saw. Use the information in Exercise 7 to help you.**

View from Tower Bridge, London

Hi!
We're in London, it's HUGE! We went on a tour of Tower Bridge today ... it's amazing. We ...

____
____
____
____
____

See you soon,

____

Published by LJS Postcards Ltd

Josh Brown
6 Station Road
Albridge
UVW 6RT
D5616

Writing Challenge 4

1 **Read the postcard. Add punctuation marks when you see ▯ .**

Hi Tom ▯

How are you ▯ Did you get my email ▯

We're staying in Cambridge for a week ▯ It ▯ s an amazing city ▯ We went on a boat trip yesterday ▯ It was great fun but I got VERY wet ▯ There are a lot of beautiful buildings and gardens here and I ▯ m taking thousands of photos with dad ▯ s new camera ▯ This morning ▯ we went to the Fitzwilliam Museum ▯ it was quite interesting but I prefer the shops ▯ There ▯ s a really good market here ▯ I want to go there this afternoon ▯

See you soon ▯ Katie

Tom Granger
5 Willow Road
Lanchester
SP2 2AL

2 **Imagine you are in your favourite place. Write a postcard to a friend. Answer these questions.**

- Where are you?
- Why do you like it there?
- What did you do yesterday?
- What do you want to do next?

Printed by PE Postcard Services Ltd

S2384

Understanding Grammar: Future Conditional

Grammar Reference, page 111

☆ **1 Put the words in the correct order to make sentences. Remember punctuation!**

1 be / you / late / you'll / if / tired / go / to / tomorrow / bed
If you go to bed late, you'll be tired tomorrow.
2 won't / the / weather's / camping / if / we / go / bad
______
3 parents / late / will / get / my / I'm / angry / if
______
4 you / the / bus / do / miss / what / if / you / will
______
5 we / the / competition / be / amazing / will / if / it / win
______
6 she / if / study / she / won't / anything / doesn't / learn
______

☆☆ **2 Choose the correct form of the verbs.**

1 If he *doesn't pass*/*won't pass* the exam, he *try*/*'ll try* again.
2 We *'ll phone*/*phone* you if the train *is*/*will be* late.
3 If nobody *will want*/*wants* to go out, we *will watch*/*watch* DVDs at home.
4 Kate *won't go*/*doesn't go* to the party if you *won't invite*/*don't invite* her.
5 If you *will be*/*are* in the team on Saturday, I *'ll come*/*come* and watch.
6 I *'ll be*/*be* worried if he *won't phone*/*doesn't phone* soon.

☆☆☆ **3 Complete the dialogues with the correct form of the verbs in brackets.**

A What time [1] *will you get* (you / get) home tomorrow?
B If [2] ______ (I / not have to) stay for orchestra, [3] ______ (I / get) home at about 4.
A When [4] ______ (your brother / be) eighteen?
B In July. [5] ______ (He / have) a big party – if dad [6] ______ (pay) for it!
A [7] ______ (you / go) to university if you [8] ______ (pass) your exams?
B Maybe. If [9] ______ (I / not / decide) to get a job, [10] ______ (I / study) something, somewhere!

☆☆☆ **4 Write Future Conditional sentences about the pictures. Use the verbs in brackets.**

1 (eat / be sick)
If he eats another burger, he'll be sick.

2 (not look out / have wet feet)
______

3 (see / arrest)
______

4 (not practise / not pass his music exam)
______

Language Check 8

Vocabulary

1 Complete the sentences. Use *go* or *play* and the words in the box.

camping cycling sailing skiing ~~swimming~~ volleyball

You need a swimming pool to go swimming.

1 You need a bike to ________________ .
2 You need snow to ________________ .
3 You need a ball to ________________ .
4 You need a tent to ________________ .
5 You need a boat to ________________ .

/ 5

2 Complete the adjectives.

I don't like coffee. It's horrible.

1 Our new sofa is very comfort________ .
2 This road is very danger________ .
3 It's a beaut________ day!
4 Our new dog is really act________ !
5 I'd like to be fam________ one day.

/ 5

Grammar

3 Look at Tom's diary for next week. Complete the sentences with the verbs in the correct form of *be going to* or the Present Continuous.

Monday	music lesson 5 p.m.
Tuesday	some time today, get a birthday present for Lucy. meet her at 7 outside cinema
Wednesday	dentist's 2.30
Thursday	study for maths exam!!!!
Friday	

On Monday he's having a music lesson at 5 p.m.

Some time on Tuesday he [1] ________ (get) a birthday present for Lucy. Then he [2] ________ (meet) her at 7.

On Wednesday he [3] ________ (go) to the dentist's at 2.30.

On Thursday and Friday he [4] ________ (study) for his maths exam.

(2 points for each question) / 8

4 Write sentences in the Future Conditional.

If / I / have / enough money / go on holiday
If I have enough money, I'll go on holiday.

1 I / be / amazed / if / our team / win

____

2 you / have / a pizza / if / I / pay / ?

____

3 Ben / not / be / happy / if / we / eat / his crisps

____

4 If / he / not / relax / he / be / ill

____

5 If / you / finish / your homework / you / come out / ?

____

6 If / you / pass / your exams / we / buy / you / a new laptop.

____

(2 points for each question) / 12

Key Expressions

5 Write advice for these people. Use *should* or *shouldn't*.

'I'm tired.' You should go to bed early tonight.

1 'I'm bored.'

____

2 'I've eaten five packets of crisps.'

____

3 'I can't understand my science homework.'

____

4 'I haven't got any money.'

____

5 'I've lost my friend's favourite CD.'

____

/ 5

What's your score?

Module 8

- Vocabulary
- Grammar
- Key Expressions

/ 35

This is easy.
I need more practice.
This is difficult.

Wordlist

Get Ready

Verbs

cook	verb	/kʊk/
count	verb	/kaʊnt/
draw	verb	/drɔː/
kiss	verb	/kɪs/
run	verb	/rʌn/
play	verb	/pleɪ/
sing	verb	/sɪŋ/
swim	verb	/swɪm/
touch	verb	/tʌtʃ/
write	verb	/raɪt/

Objects

digital camera	noun	/ˌdɪdʒɪtl ˈkæmərə/
drums	noun	/drʌmz/
guitar	noun	/gɪˈtɑː/
MP3 player	noun	/ˌem piː ˈθriː ˌpleɪə/
laptop	noun	/ˈlæptɒp/
mobile phone	noun	/ˌməʊbaɪl ˈfəʊn/
skateboard	noun	/ˈskeɪtbɔːd/

Places

bank	noun	/bæŋk/
bowling alley	noun	/ˈbəʊlɪŋ ˌæli/
cinema	noun	/ˈsɪnəmə/
clothes shop	noun	/ˈkləʊðz ʃɒp, ˈkləʊz-/
gym	noun	/dʒɪm/
hospital	noun	/ˈhɒspɪtl/
hotel	noun	/həʊˈtel/
ice rink	noun	/ˈaɪs rɪŋk/
newsagent's	noun	/ˈnjuːzˌeɪdʒənts/
park	noun	/pɑːk/
post office	noun	/ˈpəʊst ˌɒfɪs/
school	noun	/skuːl/
shopping centre	noun	/ˈʃɒpɪŋ ˌsentə/
snack bar	noun	/ˈsnæk bɑː/
sports centre	noun	/ˈspɔːts ˌsentə/
supermarket	noun	/ˈsuːpəmɑːkət/
swimming pool	noun	/ˈswɪmɪŋ puːl/

Rooms

bathroom	noun	/ˈbɑːθrʊm, -ruːm/
bedroom	noun	/ˈbedrʊm, -ruːm/
kitchen	noun	/ˈkɪtʃən/
living room	noun	/ˈlɪvɪŋ ruːm, rʊm/

Furniture

armchair	noun	/ˈɑːmtʃeə/
bed	noun	/bed/
bookcase	noun	/ˈbʊk-keɪs/
chair	noun	/tʃeə/
cupboard	noun	/ˈkʌbəd/
desk	noun	/desk/
sofa	noun	/ˈsəʊfə/
table	noun	/ˈteɪbəl/
wardrobe	noun	/ˈwɔːdrəʊb/

Things

bath	noun	/bɑːθ/
computer	noun	/kəmˈpjuːtə/
cooker	noun	/ˈkʊkə/
fridge	noun	/frɪdʒ/
lamp	noun	/læmp/
shower	noun	/ˈʃaʊə/
sink	noun	/sɪŋk/
television	noun	/ˈteləˌvɪʒən, ˌteləˈvɪʒən/
toilet	noun	/ˈtɔɪlət/
washing machine	noun	/ˈwɒʃɪŋ məˌʃiːn/

Module 1

Hobbies and Interests

art	noun	/ɑːt/
chess	noun	/tʃes/
computers	noun	/kəmˈpjuːtəz/
dancing	noun	/ˈdɑːnsɪŋ/
fashion	noun	/ˈfæʃən/
music	noun	/ˈmjuːzɪk/
photography	noun	/fəˈtɒgrəfi/
reading	noun	/ˈriːdɪŋ/
science	noun	/ˈsaɪəns/
skateboarding	noun	/ˈskeɪtbɔːdɪŋ/
sport	noun	/spɔːt/

Communication

send	noun	/send/
card	noun	/kɑːd/
e-card	noun	/ˈiː kɑːd/
email	noun	/ˈiːmeɪl/
letter	noun	/ˈletə/
text	noun	/tekst/
use	noun	/juːs/
a landline	noun	/ə ˈlændlaɪn/
a mobile	noun	/ə ˈməʊbaɪl/
Skype	noun	/skaɪp/
a social networking site	noun	/ə ˌsəʊʃəl ˈnetwɜːkɪŋ ˌsaɪt/

Personality Adjectives

friendly	adjective	/ˈfrendli/
funny	adjective	/ˈfʌni/
hard-working	adjective	/ˌhɑːd ˈwɜːkɪŋ/
helpful	adjective	/ˈhelpfəl/
honest	adjective	/ˈɒnəst/
kind	adjective	/ˈkaɪnd/
lazy	adjective	/ˈleɪzi/
moody	adjective	/ˈmuːdi/
organised	adjective	/ˈɔːgənaɪzd/
outgoing	adjective	/ˌaʊtˈgəʊɪŋ/
patient	adjective	/ˈpeɪʃənt/
shy	adjective	/ʃaɪ/
untidy	adjective	/ʌnˈtaɪdi/

Adjectives

beautiful	adjective	/ˈbjuːtɪfəl/
excellent	adjective	/ˈeksələnt/
famous	adjective	/ˈfeɪməs/
great	adjective	/greɪt/
historic	adjective	/hɪˈstɒrɪk/
lovely	adjective	/ˈlʌvli/

Module 2

Jobs

dentist	noun	/ˈdentɪst/
doctor	noun	/ˈdɒktə/
electrician	noun	/ɪˌlekˈtrɪʃən, ˌelɪk-/
hairdresser	noun	/ˈheəˌdresə/
lorry driver	noun	/ˈlɒri ˌdraɪvə/
mechanic	noun	/mɪˈkænɪk/
office worker	noun	/ˈɒfɪs ˌwɜːkə/
plumber	noun	/ˈplʌmə/
secretary	noun	/ˈsekrətəri, -ˌteri/
shop assistant	noun	/ˈʃɒp əˌsɪstənt/
taxi driver	noun	/ˈtæksi ˌdraɪvə/
teacher	noun	/ˈtiːtʃə/
vet	noun	/vet/

Food and Drink

burger	noun	/ˈbɜːgə/
cheese	noun	/tʃiːz/
chips	noun plural	/tʃɪps/
cola	noun	/ˈkəʊlə/
fish	noun	/fɪʃ/
fruit	noun	/fruːt/
hot dog	noun	/ˈhɒt dɒg/
ice cream	noun	/ˌaɪs ˈkriːm/
kebab	noun	/kɪˈbæb/
meat	noun	/miːt/
milk	noun	/mɪlk/
orange juice	noun	/ˈɒrəndʒ ˌdʒuːs/
pizza	noun	/ˈpiːtsə/
salad	noun	/ˈsæləd/
sandwich	noun	/ˈsænwɪdʒ/
vegetables	noun plural	/ˈvedʒtəbəlz/
water	noun	/ˈwɔːtə/
yoghurt	noun	/ˈjɒgət/

Module 3

Months

January	noun	/ˈdʒænjuəri, -njʊri/
February	noun	/ˈfebruəri, ˈfebjʊri/
March	noun	/mɑːtʃ/
April	noun	/ˈeɪprəl/
May	noun	/meɪ/
June	noun	/dʒuːn/
July	noun	/dʒʊˈlaɪ/
August	noun	/ˈɔːgəst/
September	noun	/sepˈtembə/
October	noun	/ɒkˈtəʊbə/
November	noun	/nəʊˈvembə, nəˈv-/
December	noun	/dɪˈsembə/

Common Verbs

get	verb	/get/
go	verb	/gəʊ/
have	verb	/həv, hæv/
leave	verb	/liːv/
read	verb	/riːd/
see	verb	/siː/
wear	verb	/weə/
write	verb	/raɪt/

Module 4

Creatures

alien	noun	/ˈeɪliən/
fairy	noun	/ˈfeəri/
ghost	noun	/gəʊst/
hobbit	noun	/ˈhɒbɪt/
mermaid	noun	/ˈmɜːmeɪd/
sea monster	noun	/ˈsiː ˌmɒnstə/
vampire	noun	/ˈvæmpaɪə/
werewolf	noun	/ˈweə-, ˈwɪəwʊlf/
witch	noun	/wɪtʃ/
yeti	noun	/ˈjeti/
zombie	noun	/ˈzɒmbi/

Senses

hear	verb	/hɪə/
see	verb	/siː/
smell	verb	/smel/
taste	verb	/teɪst/
touch	verb	/tʌtʃ/

Adjectives

dark	adjective	/dɑːk/
dirty	adjective	/ˈdɜːti/
enormous	adjective	/ɪˈnɔːməs/
horrible	adjective	/ˈhɒrəbəl/, -ɪbəl
huge	adjective	/hjuːdʒ/
long	adjective	/lɒŋ/
round	adjective	/raʊnd/
scary	adjective	/ˈskeəri/
strange	adjective	/streɪndʒ/

Module 5

Performers

acrobat	noun	/ˈækrəbæt/
actor	noun	/ˈæktə/
actress	noun	/ˈæktrəs/
clown	noun	/klaʊn/
comedian	noun	/kəˈmiːdiən/
dancer	noun	/ˈdɑːnsə/
gymnast	noun	/ˈdʒɪmnæst, -nəst/
human statue	noun	/ˌhjuːmən ˈstætʃuː/
ice skater	noun	/ˈaɪs ˌskeɪtə/
juggler	noun	/ˈdʒʌglə/
magician	noun	/məˈdʒɪʃən/
musician	noun	/mjuːˈzɪʃən/
singer	noun	/ˈsɪŋə/
storyteller	noun	/ˈstɔːriˌtelə/
trapeze artist	noun	/trəˈpiːz ˌɑːtəst/

Module 6

Appearance (1)

General

fat	adjective	/fæt/
good-looking	adjective	/ˌɡʊd ˈlʊkɪŋ/
plump	adjective	/plʌmp/
pretty	adjective	/ˈprɪti/
short	adjective	/ʃɔːt/
slim	adjective	/slɪm/
tall	adjective	/tɔːl/
thin	adjective	/θɪn/

Eyes

blue	adjective	/bluː/
brown	adjective	/braʊn/
green	adjective	/ɡriːn/
grey	adjective	/ɡreɪ/

Hair colour

black	adjective	/blæk/
blond	adjective	/blɒnd/
brown	adjective	/braʊn/
dark	adjective	/dɑːk/
fair	adjective	/feə/
grey	adjective	/ɡreɪ/
red	adjective	/red/
white	adjective	/waɪt/

Hair style

curly	adjective	/ˈkɜːli/
long	adjective	/lɒŋ/
short	adjective	/ʃɔːt/
shoulder-length	adjective	/ˈʃəʊldə leŋθ/
straight	adjective	/streɪt/

Age

Age		**/eɪdʒ/**
young	adjective	/jʌŋ/
teenager	noun	/ˈtiːneɪdʒə/
middle-aged	adjective	/ˌmɪdl ˈeɪdʒd/
old	adjective	/əʊld/

Other

braces	noun	/ˈbreɪsɪz/
earrings	noun	/ˈɪərɪŋz/
glasses	noun	/ˈɡlɑːsɪz/

Appearance (2)

change your hairstyle	phrase	/ˈtʃeɪndʒ jə ˌheəstaɪl/
cut your hair	phrase	/ˈkʌt jə ˌheə/
dye your hair	phrase	/ˈdaɪ jə ˌheə/
grow your hair	phrase	/ˈɡrəʊ jə ˌheə/
grow a beard	phrase	/ˈɡrəʊ ə ˌbɪəd/
lose weight	phrase	/ˈluːz ˌweɪt/
paint your nails	phrase	/ˈpeɪnt jɛ ˌneɪlz/
put on weight	phrase	/ˈpʌt ɒn ˌweɪt/
shave your legs	phrase	/ˈʃeɪv jə ˌlegz/
shave your head	phrase	/ˈʃeɪv jə ˌhed/
wear make-up	phrase	/ˌweə ˌmeɪkʌp/

Clothes

Clothes		**/kləʊðz, kləʊz/**
baseball cap	noun	/ˈbeɪsbɔːl kæp/
boots	noun	/buːts/
hoodie	noun	/ˈhʊdi/
jacket	noun	/ˈdʒækət/
jeans	noun	/dʒiːnz/
jumper	noun	/ˈdʒʌmpə/
skirt	noun	/skɜːt/
top	noun	/tɒp/
tracksuit	noun	/ˈtræksuːt, -sjuːt/
trainers	noun	/ˈtreɪnəz/
T-shirt	noun	/ˈtiː ʃɜːt/
woollen hat	noun	/ˌwʊlən ˈhæt/

Adjectives

baggy	adjective	/ˈbæɡi/
tight	adjective	/taɪt/
dark	adjective	/dɑːk/
light	adjective	/laɪt/
long	adjective	/lɒŋ/
short	adjective	/ʃɔːt/

Module 7

Technology (1)

Blu-ray disc (or BD)	noun	/ˈbluː reɪ ˌdɪsk/
Blu-ray player	noun	/ˈbluː reɪ ˌpleɪə/
digital camera	noun	/ˌdɪdʒɪtl ˈkæmərə/
flat screen TV	noun	/ˌflæt skriːn tiː ˈviː/
GPS	noun	/ˌdʒiː piː ˈes/
handheld or palm computer	noun	/ˌhændheld kəmˈpjuːtə, ˌpɑːm-/
home cinema system	noun	/ˌhəʊm ˈsɪnəmə ˌsɪstəm/
interactive touch table	noun	/ˌɪntəræktɪv ˈtʌtʃ ˌteɪbəl/
laptop	noun	/ˈlæptɒp/
memory stick	noun	/ˈmeməri stɪk/
mobile charger	noun	/ˈməʊbaɪl ˌtʃɑːdʒə/
mobile with video camera	noun	/ˌməʊbaɪl wɪð ˈvɪdiəʊ ˌkæmərə/
pen drive	noun	/ˈpen draɪv/
tablet computer	noun	/ˈtæblət kəmˈpjuːtə/
watch phone	noun	/ˈwɒtʃ fəʊn/
wi-fi	noun	/ˈwaɪ faɪ/
wireless headset	noun	/ˌwaɪələs ˈhedset/

Materials and Technology (2)

battery	noun	/ˈbætəri/
metal	noun	/ˈmetl/
signal	noun	/ˈsɪɡnəl/
solar power	noun	/ˌsəʊlə ˈpaʊə/
wood	noun	/wʊd/

Module 8

Holiday Activities

go:	verb	/ɡəʊ/
camping	noun	/ˈkæmpɪŋ/
cycling	noun	/ˈsaɪklɪŋ/
fishing	noun	/ˈfɪʃɪŋ/
hiking	noun	/haɪkɪŋ/
sailing	noun	/ˈseɪlɪŋ/
sightseeing	noun	/ˈsaɪtˌsiːɪŋ/
skiing	noun	/ˈskiːɪŋ/
snorkelling	noun	/ˈsnɔːkəlɪŋ/
surfing	noun	/ˈsɜːfɪŋ/
swimming	noun	/ˈswɪmɪŋ/
go to:	verb	/ˈɡəʊ tʊ/
an amusement park	noun	/ən əˈmjuːzmənt pɑːk/
the beach	noun	/ðə ˈbiːtʃ/
the mountains	noun	/ðə ˈmaʊntənz/
a swimming pool	noun	/ə ˈswɪmɪŋ puːl/
a water park	noun	/ə ˈwɔːtə pɑːk/

play:	verb	/pleɪ/
football	noun	/ˈfʊtbɔːl/
tennis	noun	/ˈtenɪs/
volleyball	noun	/ˈvɒlibɔːl/
stay at:	verb	/ˈsteɪ ət/
a campsite	noun	/ə ˈkæmpsaɪt/
a hotel	noun	/ə həʊˈtel/
a youth hostel	noun	/ə ˈjuːθ ˌhɒstl/

Opinion Adjectives

adventurous	adjective	/ədˈventʃərəs/
amazing	adjective	/əˈmeɪzɪŋ/
beautiful	adjective	/ˈbjuːtəfɪl/
boring	adjective	/ˈbɔːrɪŋ/
brave	adjective	/breɪv/
crazy	adjective	/ˈkreɪzi/
dangerous	adjective	/ˈdeɪndʒərəs/
enjoyable	adjective	/ɪnˈdʒɔɪəbəl/
exciting	adjective	/ɪkˈsaɪtɪŋ/
great	adjective	/greɪt/
horrible	adjective	/ˈhɒrəbəl/
lovely	adjective	/ˈlʌvli/
scary	adjective	/ˈskeəri/
wonderful	adjective	/ˈwʌndəfəl/

can → Get Ready, pages 3–10

Use

We use *can* and *can't* (+ infinitive without *to*) to talk about abilities:
I can read in English but I can't speak.

Form

Affirmative				
I/You/He/She/It/We/They			**can**	swim.
Negative				
I/You/He/She/It/We/They			**can't** (cannot)	swim.
Yes/No **questions**			**Short answers**	
Can	I/you/he/she/it/we/they	**swim**?	Yes, I/you/he/she/it/we/they **can**.	No, I/you/he/she/it/we/they **can't**.
Wh- **questions**				
What **can** you **do**?				

have got/has got

Use

We use *have got*

- to talk about possessions:

*He**'s got** a dictionary.*
*She **hasn't got** a Workbook.*
***I've got** two dogs and a cat.*
*My parents **have got** a small house in the countryside.*

- to talk about family, appearance, timetable:

***I've got** a brother and a sister.*
*She**'s got** a big family.*
*David**'s got** dark hair.*
*We **haven't got** maths on Monday.*
*You**'ve got** a test today.*

Form

Affirmative					
I/You/We/They He/She/It		**'ve got** (have got) **'s got** (has got)		blue eyes.	
Negative					
I/You/We/They He/She/It		**haven't got** (have not got) **hasn't got** (has not got)		a computer.	
Yes/No **questions**				**Short answers**	
Have	I/you/we/they	**got**	a tattoo?	Yes, I/you/we/they have.	No, I/you/we/they haven't.
Has	he/she/it	**got**	dark hair?	Yes, he/she/it has.	No, he/she/it hasn't.
Wh- **questions**					
What	**have**	I/you/we/they			**got**?
	has	he/she/it			**got**?

Question words

Form

Yes/No questions start with an auxiliary verb:
***Are** you Czech?*
***Do** you come from Australia?*

Wh- questions start with a question word (*What, Which, Who, When, Where, Why, How*):
***What** do you usually have for breakfast?*
***Where** are you going?*

In questions about quantity, we use *How much* in front of uncountable nouns and *How many* in front of countable nouns:
***How much** sugar do you put in your tea?*
***How many** good friends do you have?*

Questions about the subject start with *Who* or *What*. The word order is like an affirmative sentence:
***Who bought** this cake?*
***What happened** to you?*

Compare questions about the subject with questions about the object:
Peter (subject) likes Mike (object).
Who likes Mike? → *Peter.*
Who does Peter like? → *Mike.*

there is/are with *some* and *any*

Use

We use *there is* and *there are* to say that something is or is not in a particular place:
There's *a photo of a film star on page 37.*
There aren't *any texts about animals in this book.*
There isn't *any good music on the radio.*
There's *a bar on the corner.*
There are *some new CDs.*
There are *police officers outside.*

Form

Affirmative		
There's (is) a good shopping centre. **There are** some nice snack bars.		
Negative		
There isn't (is not) an information centre. **There aren't** (are not) any youth clubs.		
***Yes/No* questions**	**Short answers**	
Is there a cinema? **Are there** any skateboard parks?	Yes, **there is**. Yes, **there are**.	No, **there isn't**. No, **there aren't**.
***Wh-* questions**		
What shops **are there**?		

Comparatives and Superlatives

Use

To compare people or things, we use the comparative form of the adjective (*bigger, higher, more beautiful, more enjoyable*) and *than*:
She is ***taller than*** *me, but I am* ***more intelligent than*** *her.*

To say that one person or thing in a group is unique, we use the superlative form of the adjective: *the biggest, the highest, the most enjoyable*:
Who is ***the fastest*** *runner in your class?*

Form

	Adjective	Comparative	Superlative
One syllable ending with a consonant	cheap	cheap**er**	**the** cheap**est**
	old	old**er**	**the** old**est**
One syllable ending with *e*	nice	nice**r**	**the** nice**st**
	white	white**r**	**the** white**st**
One syllable with a short vowel + one consonant	fat	fat**ter**	**the** fat**test**
	sad	sad**der**	**the** sad**dest**
Two syllables ending in *y*	pretty	pretti**er**	**the** pretti**est**
	trendy	trendi**er**	**the** trendi**est**
Two or more syllables	attractive	**more** attractive	**the most** attractive
	comfortable	**less** comfortable	**the least** comfortable
Irregular	good	**better**	**the best**
	bad	**worse**	**the worst**

1 Write true sentences with the words in the table.

I My parents My brother My sister My best friend My grandmother My grandfather	can can't	swim. play tennis. understand animals. speak English. play the guitar. repair a bike. make pizza. dance salsa.

1 ______________________

2 ______________________

3 ______________________

4 ______________________

5 ______________________

2 Complete the dialogue with the correct forms of *have got*.

A 1 *Have* you 2 *got* a dictionary? I 3 ________ 4 ________ mine today.

B No, I 5 ________ . Maybe Mike or Joe 6 ________ 7 ________ one.

A No, they 8 ________ 9 ________ English today.

B 10 ________ our English teacher 11 ________ lessons today? I'm sure she 12 ________ 13 ________ a dictionary.

A You're right. We 14 ________ 15 ________ a lesson with her this afternoon. I'll ask her.

3 **Put the words in the correct order to make questions.**

1 are / for / what / looking / you / ?
What are you looking for?
2 did / money / she / find / where / this / ?
______
3 home / have / why / they / early / come / ?
______
4 always / do / go / to / you / seaside / the / summer / in / ?
______
5 have / how / time / we / to / do / got / the / much / test / ?
______
6 green / whose / shoes / these / are / ?
______
7 going / why / are / new / you / to / buy / a / mobile / ?
______
8 school / when / he / start / usually / does / ?
______
9 are / listening / you / music / to / whose / ?
______
10 Britain / did / World / Cup / when / the / win / last / ?
______

4 **Read the sentences, then write questions for the answers.**

- Tom sold his house.

1 What *did Tom sell?* – His house.
2 *Who sold his house?* – Tom.

- Jill likes horror films.

3 ______ – Jill.
4 ______ – Horror films.

- David knows my phone number.

5 ______ – My phone number.
6 ______ – David.

- Sylvia won a beauty contest.

7 ______ – A beauty contest.
8 ______ – Sylvia.

- The kids have broken the window.

9 ______ – The kids.
10 ______ – The window.

5 **Complete the sentences with *is* or *are*.**

1 There *are* thirty students in my class.
2 What shops ______ there near your school?
3 There ______ a photo of John Lennon on page 31.
4 ______ there a sports centre in your town?
5 There ______ fantastic discos in Manchester.
6 ______ there oxygen on the Moon?
7 There ______ eleven players in a football team.
8 ‘______ there any hotels in your town?’ ‘Yes, there ______.’
9 There ______n't an Internet café in Summerfield, but there ______ some nice snack bars.
10 There ______ a computer in our classroom.

6 **Complete the sentences with the comparative form of the adjective in brackets.**

1 My brother is *more handsome* than yours. (handsome)
2 DiCaprio's new film is ______ than *Titanic*. (good)
3 Men are usually ______ than women. (strong)
4 Young people are ______ than old people. (fit)
5 My last essay was ______ than the others. (bad)

7 **Complete the sentences with the superlative form of the adjective in brackets.**

1 I'm the *the youngest* student in my class. (young)
2 Motorcycling is one of ______ sports. (dangerous)
3 My aunt, Celia, is ______ person in the family. (busy)
4 Tokyo is ______ city on Earth. (big)

8 **Put the adjectives in brackets in the correct form – comparative or superlative.**

1 Greta Garbo was *the most famous* actress of the 1920s and 1930s. (famous)
2 I think curly hair is ______ than straight hair. (nice)
3 Germany versus Holland was ______ match in the World Cup. (bad)
4 Comedians are often ______ than other people in real life. (sad)
5 This is ______ season in Ronaldinho's career. (successful)

Present Simple → Module 1, page 12

Use

We use the Present Simple to talk about

- things that happen regularly:

*We go **out** every weekend.*
*I **write** letters to my sister.*

- things that are true in general:

*She **likes** playing computer games.*
*It **rains** a lot in England.*

Form

Affirmative					
I/You/We/They He/She/It		**like** **likes**		texting.	
Negative					
I/You/We/They He/She/It		**don't like** doesn't like		texting.	
***Yes/No* questions**				**Short answers**	
Do	I/you/ we/they	**like**	dogs?	Yes, I/ you/we/ they **do**.	No, I/you/ we/they **don't**.
Does	he/she/ it	**like**	dogs?	Yes, he/ she/it **does**.	No, he/she/ it **doesn't**.
***Wh-* questions**					
When	**do** **does**	you he	**use**	the Internet?	

Spelling

Most verbs	+ *s*	play play**s**
do, *go* and verbs ending in *ch*, *sh*, *s* and *x*	+ *es*	do do**es** watch watch**es**
Verbs ending in consonant + *y*	change *y* to *i* and add *es*	study stud**ies**

Time adverbials

With the Present Simple we use adverbs of frequency:

0% ←→ 100%

never hardly ever sometimes often usually always

- We put them after the subject of the sentence and before the verb:

*She **often** phones her friends.*

- But we put them after the verb *be*:

*We are **never** late.*

---

1 Put the verbs in the correct form of the Present Simple.

1 I *don't go out* (not go out) with my friends during the week.
2 ________ (you / read) a lot?
3 My grandfather ________ (speak) five languages.
4 My mum ________ (not like) texting very much.
5 We ________ (spend) a lot of time playing computer games.
6 ________ (your teacher / let) students use mobiles in classes?
7 My friends ________ (not live) near the school.
8 ________ (your parents / use) the Internet?

2 Rearrange the words to make sentences.

1 never / text / I / my parents
I never text my parents.
2 you / often / newspapers / do / read / ?
____
3 to the cinema / goes / sometimes / my class / at weekends
____
4 your sister / like / getting emails / from friends / does / ?
____
5 spend / we / in the mountains / usually / our holidays
____
6 sometimes / and / write / to our grandmother / letters / my brother / I
____
7 my father / his friends / hardly ever / chats on the Net / with
____

Present Continuous → Module 2, page 22

Use

We use the Present Continuous to talk about activities happening now or around the time of speaking:
*We can't go out now, it's **raining**.*
*She's **cooking** a curry.*

Form

Affirmative				
I		**am/'m**	**cooking** lunch.	
He/She It		**is/'s**	**cooking** lunch. **raining.**	
We/You/They		**are/'re**	**having** a good time.	
Negative				
I		**am/'m not**	**cooking** lunch.	
He/She It		**is not/isn't**	**cooking** lunch. **raining.**	
We/You/They		**are not/aren't**	**having** a good time.	
***Yes/No* questions**			**Short answers**	
Am	I	**having** a good time?	Yes, I **am**.	No, **I'm not**.
Is	he/she it	**having** lunch? **raining**?	Yes, he/she/ it **is**.	No, he/she/ it **isn't**.
Are	we/you/ they	**speaking** English?	Yes, we/ you/they **are**.	No, we/ you/they **aren't**.
***Wh-* questions**				
What	are	you	cooking?	

Spelling

Most verbs	+ *ing*	listen listen**ing**
Verbs ending in consonant + *e*	take away *e* – add *ing*	drive driv**ing**
One-syllable verbs ending in a vowel + a consonant	double the consonant – add *ing*	stop stop**ping**

Time adverbials

We use the following time adverbials with the Present Continuous: *just, now, at the moment, at present.*

Their position in the sentence can be

- between *be* and the *-ing* form of the verb:
*I'm **just** writing a letter.*
- at the end of the sentence:
*We're having lunch **at the moment**.*
- at the beginning of the sentence:
***At present**, many students are revising for their exams.*

1 Write about the people in the pictures. Use the Present Continuous.

1 *They're doing judo.*

2 ______

3 ______

4 ______

5 ______

6 ______

Present Simple and Present Continuous → Module 2, page 22

Use

We use the Present Simple to talk about things that happen regularly or are generally true.

We use the Present Continuous to talk about things that are happening now or around now.

Compare these sentences:
*They **don't speak** English.* (generally – because they don't know English)
*They **aren't speaking** English.* (now – but perhaps they speak English on other occasions)
*My parents **work** hard.* (generally – they are hard-working people)
*My parents **are working** outside London this month.* (now – but they usually work in London)

1 Write true sentences with the words in the table.

My best friend I am not Are you My parents don't Do you We	doesn't play football. thinking about school? speaks German. reading this newspaper. travel a lot. like Italian food? doing homework. going to school? go out a lot? like British humour. don't eat meat. are learning Spanish. lives abroad.

____
____
____
____
____
____
____
____
____
____
____
____

2 Write the correct form of the verb in brackets. Use the Present Simple or the Present Continuous.

1 My father is a doctor. He *works* (work) in a hospital. It's Sunday today so he *isn't working* (not work).
2 There's a good match on TV, but my mum ________ (not watch) it. She ________ (not like) football.
3 My sister ________ (go) to a very good school. She is very busy now: she ________ (write) a story in French.
4 My friends ________ (play) a computer game, but I can't. I ________ (do) my homework.
5 My sister ________ (love) tomatoes. She ________ (eat) them for breakfast, lunch and dinner.
6 Look, Julia ________ (talk) on a mobile phone. Normally, she ________ (not use) it. She ________ (think) they're unhealthy.
7 Don't phone Peter. He ________ (write) the essay for tomorrow. He always ________ (do) his work at the last minute.
8 I can't believe my eyes! You ________ (wear) a suit! Normally you ________ (wear) jeans.

Articles – *a, an* or *the* → Module 2, page 29

Use and Form

We use ***a*** or ***an*** in front of singular, countable nouns. We use ***an*** in front of nouns that start with a vowel and ***a*** in front of nouns that start with a consonant:
a book / a window
an actress / an exam

We use ***a*** when it doesn't matter which person or thing we are talking about, or when we talk about the person or thing for the first time:
We need **a** *car.*
They have **a** *big garden.* (I'm talking about it for the first time.)

We use ***the*** when we talk about a person or thing again and the other person knows who or what it is:
They have a cat and a dog. **The** *dog is dangerous.*
Feed **the** *dog. She is hungry.* (our dog)

There are a lot of phrases without articles:
at night, at home, at school, in hospital, in bed, by train, by plane, by taxi, before lunch, after dinner, go to school, go to work, go home, have breakfast, have lunch.

---

1 Write *a*, *an* or nothing (—) in front of these nouns.

1	*a* table	8	______ university
2	______ exam	9	______ food
3	______ apple	10	______ cheese
4	______ water	11	______ salad
5	______ elephant	12	______ meal
6	______ restaurant	13	______ park
7	______ money	14	______ uncle

2 Complete the dialogues with *a* or *the*.

A Excuse me, where is [1] *the* railway station?
B It's in [2] ______ centre of [3] ______ town. Take [4] ______ bus or [5] ______ taxi.
A Do you live in [6] ______ flat?
B No, I live in [7] ______ house. It's very nice. [8] ______ living room is very big and it has [9] ______ fireplace. And we have [10] ______ big garden too. [11] ______ dog plays there all the time.
A He's got [12] ______ brother and [13] ______ sister, hasn't he?
B Yes, they are [14] ______ big family. They have [15] ______ cat too.

3 Add articles to these sentences if they are necessary.

1 John is at home. He's painting ↑*the* kitchen.
2 Joanna is student. She goes to school in London.
3 We often have lunch in restaurant near church.
4 What is title of new *Star Wars* film?
5 I'm going to bed. Turn TV down please.
6 I was terrified: we were in middle of forest at night.
7 Head teacher comes to work by car with friend.
8 We go to the beach in summer if weather is hot.

4 Match the words in the table to make as many expressions as possible. The article *the* is not always necessary.

by at in after before on	the	plane work taxi school home bank hospital evening morning film lunch midnight lesson bed table night phone

by plane, at the table, ______________________

____

____

Past Simple → Module 3, page 32

Use

We use the Past Simple to talk about finished actions and situations in the past:
Nicole Kidman ***acted*** *in a school play.*
She ***went*** *to acting classes.*

Form

Affirmative				
I/You/He/She/It/We/They			**lived** in Paris. **saw** a horror film.	
Negative				
I/You/He/She/It/We/They		**didn't**	**study** acting.	
***Yes/No* questions**			**Short answers**	
Did	I/you/he/she/it/we/they	**like** singing? **meet** Nicole Kidman?	Yes, I/you/he/she/it/we/they **did**.	No, I/you/he/she/it/we/they **didn't**.

Spelling

Most verbs	+ *ed*	listen listen**ed**
Verbs ending in *e*	+ *d*	arrive arriv**ed**
Verbs ending in *y*	change *y* to *i* –add *ed*	carry carr**ied**
One-syllable verb ending in a vowel + a consonant	double the consonant – add *ed* a consonant	stop stop**ped**

Many common verbs in English are irregular. (See Irregular Verbs, Students' Book, page 112)

Time adverbials

We use these time expressions with the Past Simple:
last *year/month/week/night*
two years/five days/three weeks ***ago***
in *2001/the 19th century/summer*
when *I was a child, …*

---

1 Put the verbs in the correct form of the Past Simple.

1 Where *did you buy* (you / buy) those shoes?
2 My parents ____________ (travel) a lot when they ____________ (be) students.
3 I ____________ (not go) to school yesterday, I ____________ (be) ill.
4 What ____________ (the teacher / do) when she ____________ (see) you in a pub?
5 My grandmother ____________ (sing) in a group before she ____________ (marry) my grandfather.
6 In the 1920s directors ____________ (make) three or four films in one day.
7 I ____________ (meet) Simon last week and we ____________ (talk) for three hours.
8 We ____________ (not know) that the supermarket ____________ (be) closed.
9 Why ____________ (she / go) skiing? She ____________ (have) a headache.

2 Rearrange the words to make sentences.

1 mother / did / architecture / your / study / ?
Did your mother study architecture?
2 final / we / pass / test / the / didn't
____
3 did / when / first / score / Ronaldinho / his / goal / ?
____
4 when / twenty / she / she / an / Oscar / was / won
____
5 important / last / our / month / football team / matches / three / played
____
6 didn't / her / we / like / last / film
____
7 made / a / my / cake / for / Mum / delicious / birthday
____
8 give / the / did / teacher / yesterday / homework / any / us / ?
____

Past Continuous → Module 4, page 42

Use

We use the Past Continuous to talk about

- activities that continued for some time in the past:
*I **was reading** all day.*
*We **were trying** to do our homework.*
- longer activities that form a background to events:
*When I **was walking in the park**, my dog ran away.*
*It **was raining** when the match started.*

Form

Affirmative				
I/He/She We/You/They		**was reading** **were watching**	a magazine. TV.	
Negative				
I/He/She We/You/they		**wasn't drinking** **weren't studying**.	coffee.	
***Yes/No* questions**			**Short answers**	
Was **Were**	I/he/she we/you/they	**talking** on the phone? **sitting** or **standing**?	Yes, I/ he/she **was**.	No, we/ you/they **weren't**.
***Wh-* questions**				
Where	**was**	she	**staying**?	

1 Rearrange the words to make sentences.

1 talking / his / John / to / evening / friend / was / all
John was talking to his friend all evening.

2 doing / what / at / you / were / 8 o'clock / ?
____

3 friends / was / I / when / washing up / my / arrived
____

4 came in / a / were / we / test / when / the / head teacher / writing
____

5 playing / your / the / all / was / computer / brother / time / games
____

2 Complete the sentences with *was* or *were*.

1 All my friends *were* waiting on the platform.
2 The student ______ writing on the blackboard.
3 I ______ looking for my pen.
4 My sister and I ______ walking to school.
5 ______ you talking about me?
6 The fans ______ watching the match.

3 Put the verbs in the correct form of the Past Continuous.

1 I *was reading* (read) a book all night.
2 ______ (you / watch) BBC1 at 9 o'clock?
3 My dog ______ (run) after a cat when a car hit him.
4 I ______ (not play) a computer game, I ______ (work) on a project.
5 What ______ (Jane / do) last night?
6 The teachers ______ (look for) the lost student all afternoon.
7 We ______ (not have) tea at five o'clock, we ______ (do) judo.
8 Where ______ (they / sit) when you came in?
9 Mark ______ (write) an essay all afternoon. What ______ (you / do)?
10 The students ______ (fight) when the teacher came in.
11 The driver ______ (not think) about driving, he ______ (talk) on his mobile!
12 ______ (your friends / dance) all night?

Past Simple and Past Continuous → Module 4, page 43

Use

When we use the Past Simple and the Past Continuous in one sentence, the Past Continuous describes the background, and the Past Simple reports an event:
*When he **was having** lunch, he **heard** a dog outside.*
*John **phoned** when I **was watching** the Wimbledon final.*

Notice that we put a comma after the '*when*' clause when it comes first in the sentence.

a longer activity: Past Continuous

a past event: Past Simple

---

1 Complete the sentences with *did*, *was*, *were* or nothing (—).

1 *Did* you like the film?
2 They ______ not come to school yesterday.
3 The plane ______ arrived late.
4 Mike ______ thinking about the match and ______ not see the red light.
5 ______ they playing well?
6 We ______ left when the president ______ giving a speech.

2 Complete the sentences. Use the infinitive, the Past Simple or the *-ing* form.

1 When did you *come* (come) home?
2 Mark was ______ (talk) on his mobile when he ______ (see) Eve.
3 Were they ______ (listen) to your presentation or ______ (think) about their lunch?
4 I didn't ______ (work) a lot on this project. Jessica ______ (do) most of the work.
5 Brazil were ______ (play) well, but they ______ (lose) their first match.
6 Was he ______ (wait) for you at the airport when you ______ (arrive) in Moscow?

3 Put the verbs in the correct form of the Past Simple or the Past Continuous.

1 I *wasn't having* (not have) a shower when you *phoned* (phone). I *was making* (make) a sandwich.
2 ______ (you / watch) the match last night? When ______ (Beckham / score) the first goal?
3 What ______ (you / do) at 9.15 yesterday morning? ______ (you /see) the accident?
4 We ______ (have) lunch in a café when someone ______ (steal) Jake's bag.
5 I ______ (not know) my grandfather. He ______ (die) when I ______ (be) six years old.

4 Complete the story. Use the correct forms of the Past Simple or the Past Continuous.

Yesterday, we [1] *were walking* (walk) along the river when my brother, Sid, [2] ______ (see) a black bag in the water. He [3] ______ (take off) his clothes and [4] ______ (jump) into the river to get to the bag. I [5] ______ (not want) him to do it, but he wasn't scared. He [6] ______ (try) to catch the bag under the water so he I [7] ______ (not hear) the police car. Three police officers [8] ______ (get) out of the car. Sid [9] ______ (see) them when they [10] ______ (run) towards him and he [11] ______ (stop) moving. Two officers [12] ______ (catch) Sid and the third [13] ______ (take) the bag. We [14] ______ (not understand) what [15] ______ (happen). At the police station we [16] ______ (find out) that the police [17] ______ (wait) for criminals to pick up the bag. There [18] ______ (be) two million pounds inside!

some, any, a lot of, no → Module 4, page 49

Use and Form

English nouns can be countable (*a man, a table*) and uncountable (*milk, money*).

Countable nouns
- can be singular or plural: *(flower – flowers)*
- can have numbers in front of them: *(I have two cats. There are six men in the team.)*

Uncountable nouns
- have no plural form and always appear with a singular verb: *(Money isn't everything.)*
- don't appear with numbers: *(I've got some/a lot of time.)*
- don't have *a* or *an* in front of them: *(I bought bread and milk.)*

We use ***some*** and ***any*** in front of plural and uncountable nouns. We usually use ***some*** in affirmative sentences and ***any*** in questions and negative statements.

Countable nouns	Uncountable nouns
We've got **some** apples.	I need **some** money.
Do you know **any** good clubs?	Did you buy **any** meat?
I don't eat **any** cakes.	There isn't **any** cola.

We use *no* in front of uncountable and plural nouns:
I've got ***no*** *money at all.*
There are ***no*** *students in the classroom.* (*no = not any*)
I've got ***no*** *problems at all.*
*I have****n't*** *got* ***any*** *problems.*

We use *a lot of* in front of plural and uncountable nouns:
We've got ***a lot of*** *friends.*
They earn ***a lot of*** *money.*

---

1 **Write these sentences in the plural.**

1 My friend doesn't like milk.
My friends don't like milk.

2 The boy wants a sandwich and orange juice.
____

3 Our neighbour hasn't got a child.
____

4 The businessman needs time and money.
____

5 He had a sweet, but he didn't have any water.
____

6 The student is having lunch in a fast-food restaurant.
____

7 She doesn't eat meat. She's a vegetarian.
____

2 **Complete the dialogue. Use *some*, *any*, *no* or *a lot of*.**

A What do you do to keep fit?

B Well, I drink 1 *a lot of* water every day – more than 2 litres. I don't eat 2 ______ sweets and don't drink 3 ______ tea or coffee. And I spend 4 ______ time in the open air. I'm a gardener. I have 5 ______ car so I do 6 ______ walking.

A Do you do 7 ______ sports?

B I do 8 ______ sport, but not very much. There is 9 ______ gym in my area so I can't exercise regularly. And I have 10 ______ time for sport: I work a lot. But once a week I go to the swimming pool with 11 ______ friends. We always have 12 ______ fun there.

can, can't, have to, not have to → Module 5, page 52

Use

We use *can* to say that something is allowed or is possible:
*You **can** leave now.*
*In football you **can** touch the ball with your head.*

We also use *can* to talk about ability:
*I **can** swim.*

We use *can't* to say that something is not allowed or is not possible:
*You **can't** go there.*
*In football you **can't** touch the ball with your hands.*

We also use *can't* to talk about lack of ability:
*I **can't** drive.*

We use *have to* to say that something is necessary:
*You **have to** do your homework.*

We use *not have to* to say that something is not necessary:
*We **don't have to** get up early at the weekend.*

Form

After *can* and *can't* we use the infinitive without *to*:
*We **can go** now.*
*You **can't be** late.*

---

1 Complete the text. Use *to* or nothing (—).

In a library, you can't [1] ___—___ eat or drink because you have [2] ________ keep the books clean. You have [3] ________ be quiet and you can't [4] ________ listen to music. You don't have [5] ________ leave your own books at home, but you have [6] ________ tell the librarian that you want to use them. You can [7] ________ study in a library all day, but you have [8] ________ leave at night – the books have [9] ________ get some rest too!

2 Complete the sentences with *can* or *can't*.

1 You ___*can't*___ talk loudly in a library.
2 In football, players ________ touch the ball with their heads.
3 You ________ eat sweets if you want to be slim.
4 People ________ come in through the window.
5 Children ________ watch '16+' films.
6 In Canada, you ________ communicate in English or French.
7 You ________ cheat during exams.

3 Complete the sentences with *have to* or *not have to*.

1 In a pub, people ___*don't have to*___ wear formal clothes.
2 Teachers ____________ check their students' tests.
3 Sports people ____________ train every day.
4 You ____________ be very bright to use a computer.
5 Actors ____________ work from 9 to 5 every day.
6 Adults ____________ go to school anymore.

4 Complete the head teacher's speech. Use *can*, *can't*, *have to* or *not have to*.

'Welcome to our school! In this school students [1] ___*can*___ learn a lot. You [2] ________ come to classes late and you [3] ________ work systematically. You [4] ________ choose extra afternoon activities, like swimming or basketball. But you [5] ________ do sports – there's also cooking, gardening, etc. You [6] ________ also learn languages – French and German. You [7] ________ learn Russian at the moment because the teacher is ill. You [8] ________ wear a uniform, but your clothes [9] ________ be clean and tidy.'

Present Perfect → Module 6, page 63

Use

We use the Present Perfect tense to talk about past events and activities that have results or consequences now:
*The teacher **has gone** out.* (He isn't here.)
*He **hasn't cut** his hair.* (His hair is still long.)

Form

Affirmative		
I/We/You/They	**have/'ve**	**cleaned** the house. **seen** a ghost.
He/She/It	**has/'s**	**played** football. **lost** the ball.
Negative		
I/We/You/They	**have not/ haven't**	**cleaned** the house. **seen** a ghost.
He/She/It	**has not/hasn't**	**played** football. **lost** the ball.

***Yes/No* questions**			**Short answers**	
Have	I/you/we/ they	**painted** the walls? **had** lunch?	Yes, I/we/ you/they **have**.	No, I/we/ you/they **haven't**.
Has	he/she/it	**talked** to you? **built** a shelf?	Yes, he/ she/it **has**.	No, he/ she/it **hasn't**.

1 Write sentences in the Present Perfect tense. Use the ideas in the box.

break his leg   change her hairstyle clean it   not correct our tests   ~~cut her hair~~ not have breakfast   lose my key not read the papers   steal it   win the lottery

1 Mary's hair is short. She*'s cut her hair* .
2 Mike's room is very clean. He ______________ .
3 My money is gone. Someone ______________ .
4 We are very happy. We ______________ .
5 Jim is shouting. He ______________ .
6 The kids are hungry. They ______________ .
7 Dad doesn't know the news. He ______________ .
8 We don't know our grades. The teacher ______________ .
9 Gina looks terrific. She ______________ .
10 I can't open the door. I ______________ .

2 Put the verbs in the correct form of the Present Perfect.

1 *Have you finished* (you / finish) your homework?
2 Liz is at home. She ______________ (not go out) yet.
3 Look, I ______________ (buy) this new jacket.
4 I can't find my scarf. Where ______________ (you / put) it?
5 ______________ (Jane / send) you an email about her new boyfriend?
6 Ray is sad. He ______________ (not find) his dog.
7 My parents ______________ (give) me a new camera.
8 The party will be great. We ______________ (invite) all our friends.
9 I can't take my driving test. I ______________ (not learn) to park the car.
10 We ______________ (not eat) everything. There's some salad in the fridge.

must and *mustn't* → Module 6, page 69

Use

We use

- *must* when it is very important to do something, it is a rule or it is allowed.
- *mustn't* when it is very important not to do something, it is a rule or it isn't allowed.

Form

must and *mustn't* are modal verbs. We use the infinitive without *to* after modal verbs.

I must do my homework. ~~*I must to do my homework.*~~

Affirmative				
I/You/He/She/It/We/They	**must**		read the instructions.	
Negative				
I/You/He/She/It/We/They	**mustn't**		cycle without a helmet.	
***Yes/No* questions**			**Short answers**	
Must	I/you/he/she/it/we/they	go to bed?	Yes, I/you/he/she/it/we/they **must**.	No, I/you/he/she/it/we/they **mustn't**.
***Wh-* questions**				
What	**must**	I/you/he/she/it/we/they		do?

1 **There is a mistake in each sentence. Find it and correct it.**

1 Why must I ~~to~~ read the instructions?
2 He mustn't dyes his friend's hair.
3 'Must they do an allergy test?' 'Yes, they mustn't.'
4 You mustn't look after your pets. It's very important.
5 'Must she to listen to the doctor's advice?' 'Yes, she must.'
6 You must go to bed late. It's a school day tomorrow.

2 **Complete the sentences with *must* or *mustn't*.**

1 Before you use this hair gel, you *must* do an allergy test.
2 You ________ pierce your friend's ears. It's dangerous.
3 You ________ give your medicine to another person.
4 Her leg is broken! You ________ ring for an ambulance.
5 You ________ ride your bike at night without lights.
6 He wants to run a marathon. He ________ wear good trainers.

3 **Complete the second sentence so it means the same as the first.**

1 It is very important to tell your parents where you are going.
You must tell your parents where you are going.
2 Don't bring pets to school. It's a rule.
You mustn't ________________________________
3 It is very important that you don't jump into the river.
You ________________________________
4 It's a rule that students are polite to teachers.
Students ________________________________
5 It's very unkind to send horrible texts to people.
You ________________________________
6 These exams are very important so work hard.
You ________________________________

will for predictions → Module 7, page 72

Use

We use *will* and *won't* to make predictions about the future:
Your boyfriend ***will love*** *this present.*
Don't worry, you ***won't be*** *ill.*

Form

After *will* and *won't* we always use the infinitive without *to*:

Affirmative		
In the future people **will stop** going to the cinema. There **will be** more electronic equipment in our homes.		
Negative		
There **won't be** many traditional TV sets. We **won't buy** many books.		
***Yes/No* questions**	**Short answers**	
Will shopping on the Internet **become** more popular?	Yes, it **will**.	No it **won't**.
***Wh-* questions**		
Where **will** people **buy** clothes?		

---

1 Complete the sentences with *am, is, are* or *will be*.

1 Julia works very hard. She *will be* the best student next term.
2 Don't tell her that she failed the test. She ________ very upset.
3 You can't talk to Mike now. He ________ in the bathroom.
4 Phone me this evening. I ________ at home after 8 o'clock.
5 Our parents don't have any free time: they ________ very busy.
6 It's very late. We ________ very sleepy tomorrow.
7 I like our school. It ________ very nice.
8 Don't worry about the final exam: it ________ be easy.
9 I'm sure cities ________ more polluted in the future.
10 Our teacher is from Mexico. He ________ at school tomorrow.
11 Why don't you buy this jacket? It ________ really cheap.
12 Call me later, please. I ________ at the doctor's at the moment.

2 Complete the sentences with *will* or *won't*.

1 Brazil is an excellent team. I'm sure they *will* win the tournament.
2 Don't eat so many sweets! You ________ get fat.
3 Paul is ill, so he ________ come to school tomorrow.
4 The weather report is good: it ________ rain today.
5 My birthday is next week. I hope I ________ get a new CD for my reggae collection.
6 They don't like action films. They ________ enjoy *Mission Impossible 3*.
7 Adam isn't a very good student. I'm afraid he ________ pass the exam.
8 Nina is very patient, so she ________ be a great primary teacher.
9 Brian is very clever. He ________ make a lot of money in business.
10 I'm so tired, I ________ fall asleep in a minute.
11 The climbers ________ reach the top of the mountain: there's too much snow.
12 You are an excellent cook. I'm sure the dinner ________ be delicious.

Arrangements and intentions → Module 8, page 82

Use

We use *be going to* to express our intention to do something:
***I'm going to change** my hairstyle.*
*My parents **are going to move** to Italy.*

We use the Present Continuous to talk about future events that we have fixed or arranged:
***I'm starting** a new job in June.* (The arrangements have already been made.)
***We're going** to the theatre tonight.* (We've got the tickets.)

---

1 Write about the people in the pictures. Use *going to* and the ideas in the box.

interview somebody ~~look at his teeth~~ repair the car sleep write a word

1 *She's going to look at his teeth.*

2 ____________________ ____________________

3 ____________________ ____________________

4 ____________________ ____________________

5 ____________________ ____________________

2 Complete the dialogue with *be going to* (intention) or the Present Continuous (arrangement).

A [1]*Are you doing* (you / do) anything on Saturday?
B Yes, I am. I [2]__________ (meet) Peter. We [3]__________ (buy) some CDs.
A [4]__________ (you / go out) tonight too?
B No, I [5]__________ (stay) at home but I'm busy. My father [6]__________ (have) a party and a lot of people [7]__________ (come).
A What about tomorrow?
B I have to study. Don't you remember? We [8]__________ (have) a test on Friday. I [9]__________ (not go out) before the test.

3 Are these sentences about the *present* or the *future*?

1 We're learning to dance salsa. *present*
2 The teacher is giving the tests back tomorrow. __________
3 I'm going to look for a job. __________
4 Dorothy is flying to France next week. __________
5 They're not playing very well. __________
6 We're going to help you. __________

Future Conditional → Module 8, page 89

Use

We can use the Future Conditional to talk about possible future events when they depend on other future events:
*If the rain **stops**, the match **will begin**.*
*You **will get** fat if you **don't do** any sport.*

Form

If + clause	main clause
If + Present Simple, **If** you **arrive** late,	*will/won't* + infinitive without *to* they **won't let** you in.
Main clause	***if* clause**
will/won't + infinitive without *to* *I **won't go out** tonight*	*if* + Present Simple **if I have** a lot of homework.

Notice that we use a comma after the *if*-clause if it comes first in the sentence.

---

1 Choose the correct words.

1 I *cry/will cry* if I *fail/will fail* the test on Monday.
2 If we *don't/won't* do any sport, we *aren't/won't* be fit.
3 I *don't/won't* phone you if you *don't/won't* give me your phone number.
4 Stop working if your eyes *hurt/will hurt*.
5 If Mary *does/will do* everything today, she *has/will have* a free day tomorrow
6 If the weather *is/will be* good tomorrow, they *have/will have* their PE class outdoors.

2 Complete the sentences. Use the correct form of the verb in brackets.

1 If you *find* (find) my lost pen, I *will be* (be) very happy.
2 I ________ (go) on a cycling holiday if I ________ (get) a new bike.
3 If my brother ________ (go) to university next year, he ________ (move) to London.
4 We ________ (be) sad if the teacher ________ (not let) us go home early.
5 If you ________ (not stop) playing computer games, your parents ________ (be) angry.
6 My sister ________ (learn) some Spanish if she ________ (go) to Barcelona in summer.

3 Write sentences using the Future Conditional.

1 (you) go to bed early → feel good tomorrow
If you go to bed early, you will feel good tomorrow.
2 (we) not have free time → not go out
____
3 (she) not hurry → miss the bus
____
4 (it) rain → (we) watch TV at home
____
5 (they) be late for school → not run
____
6 (he) watch too much television → have problems with his eyes
____
7 (you) help me learn maths → (I) help you with English
____
8 (I) lose my mobile → (my dad) be angry
____
9 (the teacher) not come soon → (we) go home
____

Grammar Reference – Key

Page 96 – Get Ready (Revision)

Exercise 2 **3** haven't **4** got **5** haven't **6** has **7** got **8** haven't **9** got **10** Has **11** got **12** 's **13** got **14** have **15** got

Exercise 3 **2** Where did she find this money? **3** Why have they come home early? **4** Do you always go to the seaside in summer? **5** How much time have we got to do the test? **6** Whose are these green shoes? **7** Why are you going to buy a new mobile? **8** When does he usually start school? **9** Whose music are you listening to? **10** When did Britain last win the world cup?

Exercise 4 **3** Who likes horror films? **4** What does Jill like? **5** What does David know? **6** Who knows my phone number? **7** What did Sylvia win? **8** Who won a beauty contest? **9** Who has broken the window? **10** What have the kids broken?

Exercise 5 **2** are **3** is **4** Is **5** are **6** Is **7** are **8** Are / are **9** is / are **10** is

Exercise 6 **2** better **3** stronger **4** fitter **5** worse

Exercise 7 **2** the most dangerous **3** the busiest **4** the biggest

Exercise 8 **2** nicer **3** the worst **4** sadder **5** the most successful

Page 98 – Present Simple

Exercise 1 **2** Do you read **3** speaks **4** doesn't like **5** spend **6** Does your teacher let **7** don't live **8** Do your parents use

Exercise 2 **2** Do you often read newspapers? **3** My class sometimes goes to the cinema at weekends. **4** Does your sister like getting emails from friends? **5** We usually spend our holidays in the mountains. **6** My brother and I sometimes write letters to our grandmother. **7** My father hardly ever chats on the Net with his friends.

Page 99 – Present Continuous

Exercise 1 **2** She's drawing. **3** She's singing. **4** He's reading. **5** He's playing the guitar. **6** They're playing basketball.

Page 100 – Present Simple and Present Continuous

Exercise 2 **2** isn't watching / doesn't like **3** goes / 's writing **4** are playing / am doing **5** loves / eats **6** is talking / doesn't use / thinks **7** is writing / does **8** are wearing / wear

Page 101 – Articles – *a*, *an* or *the*

Exercise 1 **2** an **3** an **4** – **5** an **6** a **7** – **8** a **9** – **10** – **11** a **12** a **13** a **14** an

Exercise 2 **2** the **3** the **4** a **5** a **6** a **7** a **8** The **9** a **10** a **11** The **12** a **13** a **14** a **15** a

Exercise 3 **2** Joanna is a student. She goes to school in London. **3** We often have lunch in a restaurant near the church. **4** What is the title of the new *Star Wars* film? **5** I'm going to bed. Turn the TV down, please. **6** I was terrified: we were in the middle of the forest at night. **7** The head teacher comes to work by car with a friend. **8** We go to the beach in summer if the weather is hot.

Exercise 4 by plane/taxi, at work/school/home/midnight/night, at the bank/table, in bed/hospital, in the taxi/evening/morning/lesson, after work/school/lunch/midnight, after the film/lesson, before work/school/lunch/midnight, before the evening/morning/film/lesson, on the plane/bed/table/phone

Page 102 – Past Simple

Exercise 1 **2** travelled / were **3** didn't go / was **4** did the teacher do / saw **5** sang / married **6** made **7** met / talked **8** didn't know / was **9** did she go skiing / had

Exercise 2 **2** We didn't pass the final test. **3** When did Ronaldhino score his first goal? **4** When she was twenty she won an Oscar. **5** Our football team played three important matches last month. **6** We didn't like her last film. **7** Mum made a delicious cake for my birthday. **8** Did the teacher give us any homework yesterday?

Page 103 – Past Continuous

Exercise 1 **2** What were you doing at 8 o'clock? **3** I was washing up when my friends arrived. **4** We were writing a test when the head teacher came in. **5** Your brother was playing computer games all the time.

Exercise 2 **2** was **3** was **4** were **5** Were **6** were

Exercise 3 **2** Were you watching **3** was running **4** wasn't playing / was working **5** was Jane doing **6** were looking for **7** weren't having / were doing **8** were they sitting **9** was writing / were you doing **10** were fighting **11** wasn't thinking / was talking **12** Were your friends dancing

Page 104 – Past Simple and Past Continuous

Exercise 1 **2** did **3** – **4** was / did **5** Were **6** – / was

Exercise 2 **2** talking / saw **3** listening / thinking **4** work / did **5** playing / lost **6** waiting / arrived

Exercise 3 **2** Did you watch / did Beckham score **3** were you doing / Did you see **4** were having / stole **5** didn't know / died / was

Exercise 4 **2** saw **3** took off **4** jumped **5** didn't want **6** was trying **7** didn't hear **8** got **9** saw **10** were running **11** stopped **12** caught **13** took **14** didn't understand **15** was happening **16** found out **17** were waiting **18** were

Page 105 – *some*, *any*, *a lot of*, *no*

Exercise 1 **2** The boys want sandwiches and orange juice. **3** Our neighbours haven't got any children. **4** Businessmen need time and money. **5** They had some sweets but they didn't have any water. **6** The students are having lunch in fast-food restaurants. **7** They don't eat meat. They are vegetarians.

Exercise 2 **2** any **3** any **4** a lot of **5** no **6** a lot of **7** any **8** some **9** no **10** no **11** some **12** a lot of

Page 106 – *can*, *can't*, *have to*, *not have to*

Exercise 1 **2** to **3** to **4** – **5** to **6** to **7** – **8** to **9** to

Exercise 2 **2** can **3** can't **4** can't **5** can't **6** can **7** can't

Exercise 3 **2** have to **3** have to **4** don't have to **5** don't have to **6** don't have to

Exercise 4 **2** can't **3** have to **4** can **5** don't have to **6** can **7** can't **8** don't have to **9** have to

Page 107 – Present Perfect

Exercise 1 **2** 's (has) cleaned it **3** has stolen it **4** 've won the lottery **5** 's (has) broken his leg **6** haven't had breakfast **7** hasn't read the papers **8** hasn't corrected our tests **9** 's (has) changed her hairstyle **10** have lost my key

Exercise 2 **2** hasn't gone out **3** have bought **4** have you put **5** Has Jane sent **6** hasn't found **7** have given **8** have invited **9** haven't learnt **10** haven't eaten

Page 108 – *must* and *mustn't*

Exercise 1 **2** He mustn't ~~dyes~~ dye his friend's hair. **3** 'Must they do an allergy test?' 'Yes, they ~~mustn't~~ must.' **4** You must ~~mustn't~~ look after your pets. It's very important. **5** 'Must she ~~to~~ listen to the doctor's advice?' 'Yes, she must.' **6** You ~~must~~ mustn't go to bed late. It's a school day tomorrow.

Exercise 2 **2** mustn't **3** mustn't **4** must **5** mustn't **6** must

Exercise 3 **2** You mustn't bring pets to school. **3** You mustn't jump into the river. **4** Students must be polite to teachers. **5** You mustn't send horrible texts to people. **6** You must work hard for these exams.

Page 109 – *will*

Exercise 1 **2** 'll be **3** 's **4** 'll be **5** are **6** 'll be **7** 's **8** will **9** will be **10** 'll be **11** 's **12** 'm

Exercise 2 **2** 'll **3** won't **4** won't **5** 'll **6** won't **7** won't **8** 'll **9** 'll **10** 'll **11** won't **12** will

Page 110 – Arrangements and intentions

Exercise 1 **2** He's going to repair the car. **3** She's going to write a word. **4** He's going to sleep. **5** He's going to interview somebody.

Exercise 2 **2** 'm meeting **3** going to buy **4** Are you going out **5** 'm staying **6** is having **7** are coming **8** 're having **9** 'm not going to go out

Exercise 3 **2** future **3** future **4** future **5** present **6** future

Page 111 – Future conditional

Exercise 1 **2** don't / won't **3** won't / don't **4** hurt **5** does / will have **6** is / will have

Exercise 2 **2** 'll go / get **3** goes / 'll move **4** will be / doesn't let **5** don't stop / will be **6** will learn / goes

Exercise 3 **2** If we don't have free time, we won't go out. **3** If she doesn't hurry, she'll miss the bus. **4** If it rains, we'll watch TV at home. **5** They'll be late for school if they don't run. **6** If he watches too much television, he'll have problems with his eyes. **7** If you help me learn maths, I'll help you with English. **8** If I lose my mobile, my dad will be angry. **9** If the teacher doesn't come soon, we'll go home.